"Gouldie,

God Bless!

Dennis

Walk with Me

A Time with Christ

Dennis E. Coates

WestBow Press
PRESS
A DIVISION OF THOMAS NELSON

WestBow Press books may be ordered through booksellers or by contacting:

WestBow Press
A Division of Thomas Nelson
1663 Liberty Drive
Bloomington, IN 47403
www.westbowpress.com
1-(866) 928-1240

Because of the dynamic nature of the Internet, any web addresses or links contained in this book may have changed since publication and may no longer be valid. The views expressed in this work are solely those of the author and do not necessarily reflect the views of the publisher, and the publisher hereby disclaims any responsibility for them.

Any people depicted in stock imagery provided by Thinkstock are models, and such images are being used for illustrative purposes only.

Certain stock imagery © Thinkstock.

ISBN: 978-1-4497-3694-1 (e)
ISBN: 978-1-4497-3695-8 (sc)
ISBN: 978-1-4497-3696-5 (hc)

Library of Congress Control Number: 2012900367

Printed in the United States of America

WestBow Press rev. date:1/20/2012

To

Diane

My wife and dearest friend

Contents

Chapter 1

❦

I WALK WITH YOU

Remember how I walked with the two disciples on the way to Emmaus?[1] Remember how they didn't recognize me when I joined them? Remember how I explained to them the Scriptures that pointed to me, and yet people did not understand? Indeed, much of that walk was spent explaining things to two people who simply didn't understand what had happened or what I was about. Even when I ate with them, they didn't understand what I was doing in their midst. It was only when I entered their hearts that they began to understand. I had been preparing them for that

---

1   Luke 24:13–35
Note: Scriptural references are from *The Jerusalem Bible*, Reader's Edition, Doubleday & Company, Inc., Garden City, New York, USA, Copyright 1966, 1967, 1968.

1

moment, and when it came, the internal, risen Jesus replaced the external, risen man who had been standing before them.

And now I wish to take a similar walk with you. Take the time to be with me, listen to me, and let me take you to that same moment when I will enter your heart. Do not try to hasten the moment, for all of these things take their natural time. I will prepare you, and then the time you have spent with me in this "walk" will have been worthwhile. Right now, I would like you to be aware and realize with whom you are walking. I walk with you because I wish to talk personally with you now.

As we begin, this is a time for you, like the two on the road to Emmaus, to listen to me and try to understand what I am explaining to you. I know that you will have questions and responses as we proceed, but let me do the talking in this initial part of our time together. I wish to set the stage for what I will say later.

When I met the two men on the road, they were very sad and bewildered. They wondered how my life could have ended in such a miserable manner. Still, they had heard the report claiming someone had seen me that Sunday morning, but they didn't know what to make of it all. They were not part of the group that I had told I would rise again, and so they weren't expecting such an event. And they were confused about what would happen now. What would happen to the work I had begun? It had seemed to be going well, and I had gathered a large following. What was to happen to all these people who had placed their belief in me? And then there was the simple fact that they didn't really understand what I had been proclaiming to everyone, namely that the kingdom of God was near.

So to begin our time together, I'd like to recall a few of the things I told my followers at the time. This is really the starting point for what I have to say to you now, and I'll elaborate further as we move forward.

First, I'd like to comment on what I had told everyone about the reason I came. I told people that I came to proclaim the nearness of the kingdom of God. "The time has come," I said, "and the kingdom of God is close at hand. Repent, and believe the Good News."[2] I wanted people to prepare themselves so they could properly receive this kingdom and become part of it. At the time, they didn't understand what I was saying, because I chose not to tell them who I was right away. And consequently, they had to understand my statements in a more general way. From my words, they understood that God was closer than they'd thought and that the effect of God being nearer to them meant that His influence was greater than they had thought.

They had felt abandoned by God because of the Roman occupation. They assumed my meaning was that God would do something about the Romans, and this thought excited them. They became even more excited when I healed people because they saw in me a person who could back up words with action. That's why so many of my followers were revolutionaries. They envisioned my forming an army to defeat the Romans and restoring governance to the Jews. To these revolutionaries, the kingdom of God meant a restoration of the Jewish kingdom.

But what do *you* think about the kingdom of God? What do *you* think I meant by my words? Is it an earthly kingdom? Is it a heavenly kingdom? Does it have any impact on your life or the lives of those you love? Does

2   Mark 1:15

it have any relationship to the governance of your city or country? Do you think that I am going to sit on the seat of an earthly power to establish the kingdom of God on earth? Do you think the church is the kingdom of God? Or are you in a similar position to my early followers in Judea, where you're just not sure what I meant by "the kingdom of God," even though you have likely heard it explained again and again by the church?

The kingdom of God and its nearness are the essence of the gospel. That's why I begin with this in our walk together, because a clear understanding of the kingdom of God is crucial to what I want to tell you through our time together.

Remember how I described different attributes of the kingdom through various parables? Let us go back to a few of these. Recall the parable about the sower of the seeds.

"A sower went out to sow his seed. As he sowed, some fell on the edge of the path and was trampled on; and the birds of the air ate it up. Some fell on rock, and when it came up it withered away, having no moisture. Some fell among thorns and the thorns grew with it and choked it. And some seed fell into rich soil and grew and produced its crop a hundred fold. Listen, anyone, who has ears to hear." [3]

When you hear this, you see that the seed, which is the Word, is spread everywhere but that it takes "rich soil" in which to grow and bear fruit. Don't be concerned about the seed that falls elsewhere. The seed that has landed in you is the object of my comments. The kingdom comes from hearing and responding to the message. I no longer have to speak in parables because you are willing to spend

---

3   Luke 8:5–8

this time with me and let me speak to your soul. The kingdom of God is about the state of the soul, the state of the heart, mind, spirit, and will. The kingdom is about the whole person, and it is about that life with God that lasts forever.

The kingdom is first planted in the heart of the individual, because each person—one at a time—enters into relationship with God. But for the kingdom to be spread and the seed to enter other souls, those who have received the kingdom and are part of it must then spread it. It is the many who have received it who spread the seed. The mustard seed is one of the smallest of seeds, yet it grows to become the largest of trees. So too is the kingdom of God. It is like the fruit of seed entering and finding a place in receptive souls that grows until there is a resting place for all in the kingdom of God. Here, it is the many who are the fertile soil for the seed, and they in turn spread the seed.

I am the sower and the Word made flesh. My words have their origin in God, and are the spoken words of God. Through the Word God has chosen to reveal himself to humankind and how He desires to bring people to himself. The Word is the very means by which God achieves His purpose.[4] I came then as the Word of God to be spoken to all, and my words are from God, your Father: "This is my Son, the chosen one. Listen to him."[5] The truth of this

---

4   Isaiah 55:10–11: "Yes, as the rain and the snow come down from the heavens and do not return without watering the earth, making it yield and giving growth to provide seed for the sower and bread for the eating, so the word that goes from my mouth does not return empty, without carrying out my will and succeeding in what it was sent to do."

5   Luke 9:36

is in the hearing of my words, and seeing what the words produce in you.

I am the Way, the Truth, and the Life. No one can come to the Father except through me. If you know me, you know my Father too.[6] Here is the key to eternal life: to know me, and through me, my Father, your Father. The seed I spread is this knowledge. The seed I spread is the seed of the kingdom itself, where the Father reigns through love and where I am known as the one who leads to Him. It is not mere words that I spread but life. I spread eternal life with God. And when you receive this life, it spreads through you to others almost imperceptibly, bearing fruit in plenty. Make your home in me, as I make mine in you. As a branch cannot bear fruit by itself but must remain part of the vine, neither can you unless you remain in me. I am the vine, and you are the branches. Whoever remains in me and with me in Him bears fruit in plenty, for cut off from me, you can do nothing.[7]

This is the very heart of the kingdom of God: eternal life. That is what I am about and what this walk is about. Attune your ear so that everything I say to you from now on is heard in this context. Everything I say has to do with the kingdom of God in you, in the church and in the world.

With this in mind, listen to a few more parables so that they enter your consciousness now and unfold even more as we continue our walk together.

The first is the parable of the fig tree.[8] A man had a fig tree planted in his vineyard, and he came looking for

---

6	John 14:6–7
7	John 15:4–5
8	Luke 13:6–9

fruit on it but found none. He said to the man who looked after the vineyard, "Look here, for three years now, I have been coming back to look for fruit on this fig tree and finding none. Cut it down. Why should it be taking up the ground?"

"Sir," the man replied, "leave it one more year and give me time to dig around it and manure it. It may bear fruit next year; if not, then you can cut it down."

The kingdom is to be filled with fig trees bearing fruit. You are one of these fig trees meant to be healthy and bearing fruit. What is it that prevents a fig tree from bearing fruit? Sometimes it is not properly rooted. I am the soil in which each is to be rooted. Sometimes it doesn't receive enough nourishment. My Word and my Body and Blood are the source of this nourishment. These are the means I have given you to remain rooted in me. Like a patient and nurturing gardener, I will help you to be firmly rooted in my soil.

You are part of a great enterprise that is the church. The church is as healthy as all its members, and dead members bring down the whole church. The church is to be my living body, providing the right climate for each member to grow. It is weak in this aspect at this moment in history. It needs all its members to contribute to the overall climate of love, fellowship, and right understanding that make the whole orchard healthy and fruitful. I, your Lord, need you to fulfill your part in this. The health and well-being of the whole church is essential for it to produce its best fruit in the world.

Recall the parable of the woman with the drachma.[9] What woman with ten drachmas would not, if she lost one,

---

9 Luke 15:8–10

light a lamp and sweep the house and search thoroughly till she found it? And then, when she had found it, call together all her friends and neighbors? "Rejoice with me," she would say, "I found the drachma I lost." In the same way, I tell you, there is rejoicing among the angels of God over one repentant sinner.

Do you spontaneously rejoice when a lost soul is restored to life with me? I care about the state of your heart in this matter. Only a moment's reflection is required to find if this is true of you or not. This is why I came—to save the lost, to separate myself from the flock to find the lost, and when I do, there is rejoicing in heaven, because those in heaven know the full extent of what this means to that soul. This is a state of heart I ask of you, and if this is not completely so, something is missing in your comprehension of the kingdom. This walk will be about these things as well.

Remember the parable about the hoarder. There was once a rich man who, after having a good harvest from his land, thought to himself, "What am I to do? I have not enough room to store my crops. This is what I will do: I will pull down my barns and build bigger ones and store all my grain and my goods in them, and I will say to my soul: My soul, you have plenty of good things laid up for many years to come; take things easy, eat, drink, have a good time." But God said to him, "Fool! This very night the demand will be made for your soul; and this hoard of yours, whose will it be then?" So it is when a man stores up treasure for himself in place of making himself rich in the sight of God.[10]

And so it is with you and all who are mine. This isn't about "laying up treasure" on earth, but it is about eternal life and passing that life on from one to another. It's about

---

10   Luke 12:16–21

helping others to be built up in that life and all being part of my life and that of the Father. My Father shares His life with others, as I do, and this is a key feature of eternal life. Grace cannot be stored but only passed on.[11]

But I know human nature, and I know that there is a tendency to want to play it safe. This, too, will be part of our journey, because I need you to be a generous person as my Father is a generous father.

The last parable I want you to reflect on is the parable of the bridesmaids.[11] The kingdom of heaven will be like this: Ten bridesmaids took their lamps and went to meet the bridegroom. Five of them were foolish, and five were sensible. The foolish ones did take their lamps, but they brought no oil, whereas the sensible ones took flasks of oil as well as their lamps. The bridegroom was late, and they all grew drowsy and fell asleep. But at midnight, there was a cry, "The bridegroom is here! Go out and meet him." At this, all those bridesmaids woke up and trimmed their lamps, and the foolish ones said to the sensible ones, "Give us some of your oil. Our lamps are going out." But they replied, "There may not be enough for us and you. You had better go to those who sell and buy some for yourselves." They had gone off to buy it when the bridegroom arrived. Those who were ready went in with him to the wedding hall, and the door closed. The other bridesmaids arrived later. "Lord, Lord," they said, "open the door for us!" But He replied, "I tell you solemnly I do not know you." So stay awake, because you do not know either the day or the hour.

It sounds strong, doesn't it? Do you believe that some will be left out of the kingdom, out of eternal life? I tell you solemnly this is the truth. But why is it the truth? It is

---

11   Matthew 25:1–13

because eternal life involves entry, real entry into life with God the Father and God the Son in the Holy Spirit. It is not a wishy-washy thing. It is not something extraneous or unimportant. It is the very reason for life itself. Let those who care about such things debate the justice of this, but this is what I say: I came to bring this eternal life to man. It is true that there are circumstances in people's lives that God has to take into consideration when the time comes, but don't think this is to be finessed into nothingness. It means what it says: Eternal life is for those who have entered into it. Those who have rejected it for something else are left outside the door, and when they realize what they have missed, there is weeping and gnashing of teeth.

Eternal life is the greatest treasure available to man and the very purpose for human existence. This is the last point, so take this very seriously. Ask God to give you the special grace of seriousness as we begin this walk together. I have come to you now at this moment in your life in this special and intimate way. Be with me now as we continue to talk about eternal life, your eternal life, and the eternal life of all who are in your life.

Chapter 2

~

WALK WITH ME

Remember how the two disciples told of how their hearts burned within them as I explained the scriptures to them along the way.[12] This is because they hadn't understood what it was that I was about. I had to explain to them what the prophets meant when they foretold certain things or described God's intentions in the face of certain conditions that had developed among His people. I'd like to go over some of these things with you. So I need you to walk with me just as I make this walk with you. I need you to walk with me with your heart, mind and spirit, just as those two disciples did.

---

12   Luke 24:32 "Did not our hearts burn within us as he talked to us on the road and explained the scriptures to us?"

Their hearts burned within them just because they paid attention to what I was telling them, and this at a time when they didn't even recognize me. Later, after they had realized who was speaking to them, they were able to tell the others what I had said about the scriptures, and this became part of the understanding of the early fathers of the church. And so, the things that I will now say to you need to become part of your very being, part of what motivates you, part of what you are able to explain to others, part of the gift I'm giving you to pass on to others. So walk with me as I walk with you.

Why do I begin by explaining scripture? It is because this is the path chosen for you to come to know me. And that is the means to eternal life. Know me, know my life, know my Father through me, know why I came in a personal way that changes your life, and know the power of the Holy Spirit that comes to you from my Father and me, and that makes eternal life possible for you. That is the purpose of this walk—to know me better. No matter what the level of your current relationship with me, you can always know me better. In fact, although no person can know me totally, the very nature of life with me is a growth in knowing me. And the more you know me, the more you know my Father, for my Father and I are one.

Let me begin with one of the key scriptures I explained to the two disciples, and that is the story of the flood.[13] When the flood had subsided, God said, "Never again will I curse the earth because of man, because his heart contrives evil from his infancy. Never again will I strike down everything I have done." This represents a promise by God and a covenant with man that no matter what evil was perpetrated by man, God would not destroy all

---

13   Genesis 7:17–8:22

to eradicate this evil. This was a new and everlasting covenant that God would never break. God would enter a new covenant in my blood, but this particular former covenant continues. I did not come to do away with former covenants of this order made by God.

The result of this is that all can be confident that no matter what man does to man, God is not going to eradicate that portion that is evil. Even within yourself, God will not eradicate you because of any evil that is in your heart and mind. I would say that the wheat would grow along with the weeds, and this was a reference to this covenant. So know that no matter what evil takes place and no matter who the perpetrator of the evil, God will not destroy the good with the evil; the two must reside together for the sake of the good and for the sake of the possibility that the evil can be turned to good, both for the recipient of evil and the perpetrator of evil. See this as good news for those in your life who do evil. See it as a promise of God that no person is outside the possibility of redemption, of changing his or her mind and ways. Know that no matter what you do, no matter what evil settles in your soul, God will not destroy *you* for that evil. You will have a chance to change your mind and ways.

Right after this, I told the two disciples that this covenant of God's was linked to another covenant made later to the people of Israel. "I will adopt you as my own people, and I will be your God."[14] The two disciples knew this promise of God's, but they couldn't connect it with me. They couldn't understand that what God wanted and needed to prepare man for was a personal relationship with man, like one of father and child. I told the two this, but they still couldn't

---

14   Exodus 6:7

grasp what I had to do with this covenant or why I would die a certain death. They couldn't understand that I was beginning a new covenant in my blood that ushered in this new era with God, that people would be related to God in a totally new way never before possible or available to mankind. "I will be your God" was to have new meaning and possibility for them.

Step back for a moment and reflect on what this means for you and all who would enter into this life. This was something new made possible by God through the offering of my life. This most important of all forms of life was acquired at a price in order to reveal its importance and to reveal the mind of God. In this new and eternal covenant, God was accomplishing His purpose from all time. It was this new and eternal covenant that God was preparing man to receive. Even when man turned away from Him again and again or followed Him in ways that really had nothing to do with the God and creator of man and the universe, God had a plan to give man eternal life.

Had you been born before me, you would never have known this life or the possibility of this life. "I will adopt you as my own people, and I will be your God" took on new and essential meaning about the kind of life God wished for His people. And that was the life of children of God. This is what I told the two disciples: They were to be true children of God—God was their Father, and they His beloved children. They didn't understand how this could be done, but they understood the thrust of what I was telling them.

One of the last things I explained to them was the promise made through the prophet Ezekiel: "I shall give you a new heart, and put a new spirit in you; I shall remove the heart of stone from your bodies and give you a heart of flesh instead."[15] Here was the very reason why people were created. Here was the very reason God had sought this new covenant and relationship. Man was made in the image of the Father and thus made for love. This was what I sought to reveal to man, not only that this was the very purpose of God but also this was the very divine nature God wanted man to participate in. Man cannot do this apart from God. Man by himself has such a limited understanding and capability to love, and this is what God wanted to improve, wanted to change by His own power and example. It is this new heart and spirit that is the purpose of my time with you, as it was with the two disciples on the road to Emmaus.

To have a new spirit, to have a heart that feels and is compassionate, to have a mind that understands from these vantage points—this is not something that comes from the mind of man but rather something from the mind and heart of God

How does this change of spirit, heart and mind come about?

It comes about by spending time with God, by hearing the words of God, by seeing His work among you, by absorbing His thinking as revealed in me. This is why I came—to make His presence among you visible, to make His mind and heart known to man, to make His desire for good fruit among people possible through His help. It is God and man "co-yoked" in a work of love.

Let us begin with the heart. How does one change one's heart? How does God change one's heart? Let me tell you this little story. A man had a wife and two daughters.

---

15   Ezekiel 36:26–7

One of the daughters was outgoing and friendly. The other was withdrawn and shy. The father couldn't understand how the two girls could be so different, and he wondered if there was some way he could help the younger girl overcome her shyness. He knew that it was painful for her to be with a large group of people, so having some kind of special event for her was out of the question. He wondered if having an event with her one special friend could help. After he thought about some alternatives, he realized he really didn't understand his daughter well enough to know what he could do to help her.

He had discussed this with his wife, and she, too, was hopeful they could do something for her but had no suggestions. They decided to ask her teacher for her opinion. When they met with the teacher, she told them she had noticed something about the girl that might be helpful. She had become aware that the girl was very happy when she was with a particular circle of friends at school and that what marked this group of friends was an interest in music. Most of the time they were together, they listened to a particular type of music. In doing this, she noticed they didn't have to speak too much, but they did share their enthusiasm for the music. The teacher had noticed that on an individual basis, each of the girls was shy, but when they were together, they were at ease and happy.

The parents were happy to hear that there was a setting where their daughter was more outgoing and at ease. They decided to ask her if there were any friends she'd like to have over to the house sometime, and she told them about this group of friends and their interest in this music. The parents arranged an evening devoted to this music when all her friends could come to the house. The party was held, and it was a great success. They noticed that after that party, the daughter was more outgoing and happier. Her friends were able to come and go. Even her parents became interested in the music.

This is a story of one girl's heart and how she felt in the company of people. The solution to her shyness was to provide a setting where she could "be at home" with the people she was with. She wasn't a person who could enter into long discussions, but she was a person who was "moved" by music. She found friendship with others who were similarly moved. They had a common interest and enjoyment, and the result was that all of them spontaneously enjoyed the others' company. This was an affair of the heart, and once the needs of the heart were met, each of the girls involved became happier and less shy in general.

This young girl couldn't have stated what the need of her heart was because she didn't know what that was through her thought processes. But her heart knew. And God knew. God knows the need of each human heart even when the person doesn't or when those close to him or her don't. When you think about it, you'll find that the needs of the human heart are hidden most of the time. God is the great lover and healer of the human heart. Indeed, God's first preoccupation with each person is the state of his or her heart. And so am I. That is why we begin always with the heart in this walk together.

Let us look at some of the things I said about the heart. "For where your treasure is, there will your heart be also."[16] This is the key. Here, in a simple sentence, is your ability to check where you are with God. When God says, "Set your

---

16   Luke 12:34

hearts on his kingdom first, and on his righteousness,"[17] He means that there cannot be two on the throne of the heart. It is either God, or it is something else. So it easy to see what governs your heart. I have given you a simple means to do so. What is your treasure? What is it that motivates you? What is it that gives life meaning for you? What is it that gives you joy? What is it that you sacrifice for? Is it for God or something else? A little reflection will identify what your god is, and if it is other than God, then realizing this will help you redirect your priorities.

It is the heart that is the seat of happiness in the person. God has made it so. But real happiness cannot be attained separated from God. Humans delude themselves with this idea. I don't mean people may not be comfortable or satisfied in their lives. That is not the happiness I speak of. The happiness I speak of is the happiness of God. God's happiness is true, everlasting happiness. It comes from who God is. It comes from His very nature. Sharing in the happiness of God is the source of true, eternal happiness.

Do you see what God is calling you to? It is to share in His divine nature. This is your future, and it begins in this life because of what I did for you and for all. I have opened the door to this new and eternal life, and it is there for all who would walk through that door. The first step to take in entering more deeply into this life with the Father and me is to check to make sure that God is first in your life. Everything else follows from that. "Set your hearts on his kingdom first, and on his righteousness, and all these other things will be given you as well."[18]

---

17   Matthew 6:33
18   Matthew 6:34

Next in checking out the state of your heart and its priorities is the level of your awareness of others. Doing this is also simple, because I have given you a sure method of checking this out. I was asked, "Which is the first of all the commandments?"[19] I answered, "Listen, Israel, the Lord your God is the one Lord, and you must love the Lord your God with all your heart, with all your soul, with all your mind, and with all your strength. The second is this: You must love your neighbor as yourself."[20]

You notice the first commandment from God is to love—to love God, to love yourself, and to love your neighbor as yourself. This is the key to the kingdom, the nature of the kingdom, and the nature of eternal life. Love is what God is all about, and it should be what you are all about. The first thing to be aware of—that is, after becoming aware of the level of your love of God—is your love for yourself. How can you live life fully if you don't properly love yourself, and how can you love your neighbor properly if you don't love yourself?

So what does loving yourself mean?

To love yourself means to know how God loves you. It is this awareness that allows you to love yourself properly. If loving yourself depended on how you felt about yourself, you might never come to love yourself properly. It is God who knows you thoroughly and who loves you properly. God knows the best you and the worst you, and He knows how to bring out the best you no matter what the worst you is. God knows your heart and what it is capable of. He knows what it was made for, and He knows what strength the heart properly formed

---

19   Mark 12:28
20   Mark 12:29–30

has. He knows what the well-formed heart is capable of in terms of all the others in your life and in terms of what this can bring about in the world.

You need to know better how much God loves you, and we will spend some time on this during our walk. Loving yourself comes from knowing how much God loves you and how much He wants you to be the fullest human being you can be.

When you know how much God loves you, how can you not realize that He loves all others the same and has the same desire for each person as He has for you? It is when you realize this in your soul that you become a different person toward all other people, no matter what their relationship to you, no matter what your past experience of them has been. This is the kingdom of God that God means to bring about through you and through others who have also realized what the love of God means and brings about.

This is the central feature and concern of our walk together. Long to be with me as I continue to open up the heart and mind of God.

Chapter 3

◞

SHARING A LIFE

As we continue this time together, you would do well to reflect on what it means to have me as a constant companion. This is the essence of my Lordship. It isn't that I "lord it over" anyone but rather that I become intimate friends with those who will walk with me. Sometimes I do give clear instruction on what you need to do or be in terms of your life with God, and this is as it should be. But the nature of my relationship with those who do enter into daily life with me is rather that of friendship: Lord and friend, savior and companion. This is how I want you to think of me always: friend, the great friend, the best friend. And it isn't just that I am friend but that I am *the* friend who, through our friendship, will bring you further into eternal life.

Don't think of this life as sometime far off in the future but as now, and more tomorrow, and more the next day. Friendship with me is dynamic, making possible daily exposure to divine life. What does it mean to share a life? It is really the same in nature as any good and loving relationship between human beings. Two friends speak to one another, share what is important to them, share moments of sadness and joy, share the travails of the day, help each other as needed, and promise to be there for each other when the going gets tough or when circumstances need another's thought or empathy. The primary difference in relationship with me is that I know much more than a human friend could. I know the human heart intimately, and I know what creates love and goodness in a person. I know how to help in the best way when help is needed, and I know how to correct when correction is needed. Most of all, I know the purpose and direction of life and how to point the soul toward its fulfillment in God. In sharing life with me, these are the things that you should expect to come from me, for I am your Lord and friend.

But what should I expect from you?

I'd like you to be my friend too. Does that seem odd, that I would want you to be my friend? It shouldn't. After all, what is love when you boil it down to everyday, practical reality? Is not love precisely that of being a friend? Friendship is one of the greatest defining features of love. So let us be friends. This is a covenant between you and me, a covenant of friendship. I have given my life for you, and I am giving my life to you. Be my friend and give your life to me so that I may have the freedom to lead you in a relationship of loving friendship. You will come to know that I am with you intimately and that I will lead you in your life in a way that opens all the doors available in developing you as a "God-person."

When you come to me each day, come with the expectancy of being with the greatest friend you have. When you come to me, come to me with the knowledge that you are coming into the presence of the one who loves you more than anyone and who knows you more than anyone. Come with that knowledge and expectation and confidence. And begin now to have that attitude, that point of view, that feeling of being in the best possible place on earth, that place where no enemy can assail you, no ignorance misdirect you, and no confusion lead you astray. This is our friendship, and you are my beloved.

And there is one thing more. When you are with me, you are with my Father, your Father, in far deeper ways than you could ever imagine. It is my task to bring you more deeply into the presence of my Father. Know that what I have said about my love for you is true of your Father in heaven. Know that He knows you and loves you, and that my purpose is the same as His. In entering into friendship with me, you have entered into the very life of the Trinity. There is no greater place in existence that one can enter, the very core of divine life. This is the walk I speak of. This is the life I wish to share with you. This is the life to which all are called but few enter. But you have this opportunity and privilege, and the greatest of the saints have pointed the way to this very life that they themselves participated in.

So enter our walk with these things in mind. As we begin, know that I am with you, know that my Father is with you, and know that the Holy Spirit is fully present with you now. Know that we love you. Just sit for a moment and take in that thought. *We love you. We made the universe so that this moment would be possible.* I came to make this moment possible. So know that you are totally safe in our care right now. It is divine life that we bring to you. It is divine life that you are participating in right now.

Let me speak to you now in this climate of love.

Recall the story of the woman who touched the hem of my garment and was healed.[21] Remember how just touching me brought about her healing. Here was a woman who had suffered for so many years and placed her hope in me that I could do something for her. I wasn't even aware of her presence, yet her belief and hope in me brought about a surge of healing power that changed her life. Imagine her desperation after so many years of suffering. Imagine her thoughts and feelings as she saw me in the distance. Imagine her as she made her way through the crowd to get close to me, not even to speak to me but to simply touch me.

This is the kind of expectation and hope that I'd like you to bring each day to our meeting. This is the kind of expectation you should have because I am your Lord. *Your Lord.* Whatever your hope, whatever your need, know that I will be with you as I was with this woman, except for one thing. She couldn't stay with me. She couldn't be with me each day in the way you can be. Come with the confidence she had in me and know that I know your true needs and your hope.

Recall the story of the rich young man who came to me to ask how he could enter into the life I spoke of.[22] He told me of how he had kept the commandments all his life, but I could see he was looking for the deeper life I spoke of. I looked at him with all the love that was in me, and I

---

21 Luke 8:43–8
22 Luke 18:18–23

saw in him the possibility of the life that I now offer you; however, he had an obstacle that stood between him and the freedom of this life with me. He was tied to wealth and the lifestyle that came with it. To truly be free, he had to make the decision to separate himself from that obstacle. "There is still one thing you lack. Sell all that you own and distribute the money to the poor, and you will have treasure in heaven; then come, follow me." But when he heard this, he was filled with sadness, for he was very rich and he couldn't do this thing that would have given him the life of an apostle.

How sad indeed was that young man, for he had within him the possibility of deep life with God. I was asking him to make that separation that opens the door to a deeper life with me. Scary, isn't it, this life with me? Are you, too, afraid of what I might ask of you? You should know that I will separate you from that which keeps you from entering into divine life more fully. Can you accept this? Can you look forward to it? Can you welcome this action of mine as a saving action in your life? Do you see what the outcome of this will be? It means a new life for you. It means a life of deep friendship with me. Can you make that sometimes terrifying decision to offer this to me now, not knowing what I will ask of you or when I will ask it? This is life with me, but you must know that I do all this for your best interest in terms of eternal life and in terms of building the kingdom of God on earth.

Attitude counts for so much in life with me. I look forward to being with you, and I am inviting you to have the same viewpoint when you come to be with me. Here are a few other dispositions to practice when you come to be with me.

Recall again the story of the woman who swept her place as she looked for the lost coin.[23] "'Rejoice with me,' she would say, 'I have found the drachma I lost.' In the same way, I tell you, there is rejoicing among the angels of God over one repentant sinner." Here is another attitude to cultivate when you prepare yourself to be with me. Know that I am the one who loves sinners. Know that I am the one who knows what I am "saving" them from. I am the one who came for them.

This is my point here: Know that there is no comparison to life with me and to life without me. See yourself as privileged in the sense that you know who I am and why I came. See yourselves as "go-betweens" between me and others I seek who don't know me at all or as well as they could. See yourself as my eyes and ears, my hands and feet to take me to others. Come to that point of view this woman had in seeking what was lost. This is my principal work, and it is your work as well, because you are "another me" in the world.

Because you know me and are attached to me and because you have my life in you, you are another me in the world. Even if you are fearful about this idea, you must come to know that even spending this time with me will "rub off" on you and that you will become more like me as time goes by, and when this happens, this love for those who are lost will become second nature to you just like breathing in and breathing out.

Here is another valuable story in which you can immerse yourself and glean its meaning. It is the story of the woman at the well.[24] It is a story of coming to worship in spirit and truth. This is the part of the story I would emphasize to

---

23   Luke 15:8–10
24   John 5:4–42

you now. To know me truly is to know the ultimate truth in life. To know me and to love me is to come to an adoration derived from love, and when this occurs, you have come to worship me in spirit and in truth.

It is this honesty I want from you and from all my followers. I am not looking for vain repetitions, idle chatter, or "going through the motions" as though I don't know what is really going on with you. If you become bored, tell me about that feeling and ask for my help in being renewed. If you have lost focus, become aware of it and come back to me for fruitful time with me. Pester me until you are satisfied with our walk. Don't fall away from me and accept that you had to part with me. Do your part to resolve whatever is making your walk with me dim. Don't settle for anything less than worshipping my Father and me in spirit and in truth.

One last story to recall is the story of Nicodemus.[25] You must read this carefully if you are to understand what I told Nicodemus. He was a man of learning and knew the law and the spirit of his faith. He came to me because I puzzled him, and he would not be content until I explained to him what I was about in terms he could understand. It was not his fault that he couldn't understand me. I was bringing something new into the world. I told him what I later told the Samaritan woman but in different words.

He was a Pharisee and taking all the actions required by precept was important to him, as he had been taught and had practiced. He was a faithful Pharisee and a good man of God. He wanted to be faithful. He saw me as a man of God, and he wanted to be clear about what I was

---

25   John 3:1–21

teaching. He had heard me say that it was not sacrifice that God wanted but faithfulness. I told the Samaritan woman the same thing using the terms "in spirit and in truth." It isn't vain practices that God is looking for, but something that comes from the heart and soul of man.

It is something that comes from God. It is now that I told him this stunning truth: Unless a man is born through water and the Spirit, he cannot enter the kingdom of God: what is born of the flesh is flesh; what is born of the Spirit is spirit. Do not be surprised when I say, "you must be born from above."[26]

And to you, I say, "Do not make the mistake that life with me can come from anything you do or can do." This is God's project, not yours. This is God's power at work to give you life in and through Him. You can do things to prevent entry into this life. You can leave by your own will or negligence, but you cannot create it, mold it, or manipulate it. You are born from above, and this is the great mystery of God's saving action that you must rejoice in. Nicodemus continued to be confused by what I had said, and it wouldn't be until the coming of the Spirit at Pentecost that he would fully understand. But you know what I am saying, and I want you to rejoice and be filled with joy at the life you are part of. This attitude comes from knowing the depth of the life that is in God.

As you walk with me, as you allow me to speak to your heart and soul, you will come to understand with your mind and your whole being what life with me means. You don't have to be anxious. You don't have to be impatient. You don't have to be anything but honest in your life with me. "Follow me" means to enter into this life with me and

26   John 3:5–7

to be compliant with what I am doing for you and in you. Let me do the work; I know where to lead you. Let me be the builder of your faith and the builder of the kingdom in you. Then you, in turn, will become a builder of what I came to build, namely, the kingdom of God on earth.

This is sharing my life, sharing my mission, sharing in the very life of the Father, Son, and Holy Spirit. You will come to see that this is the fullest, most abundant life imaginable. Come follow me and be with me in joy and thanksgiving each day. This is what our walk is about.

Chapter 4

❧

ABOUT MY FATHER

My primary task in our walk is to bring you closer to God, your Father. He and I are one, and I alone know Him in a way that I can reveal Him to others. Would it make any sense that we spend this time together and I not do this? It is not even the fact that I give you information about Him, but it is more that you come to know and love Him more. This is the touchstone of our time together, the "proof" that our time together is producing good fruit. This is the real test of the nature of eternal life.

Let me explain it this way: When you arrive in heaven and are in the very presence of God face-to-face, you will be filled with love for Him. Loving will be your nature then, as it is God's nature, and this is the nature of heaven.

Life with me now means to come to share in a foretaste of the life and love that is in heaven. How will I bring this foretaste of heaven about in you? It will be through sharing with you my own love for the Father, and it will be through your own experience of His love for you that I will make Him known to you. In these two ways, you will come to love the Father more and more, and you will come to know the joy of the Father and the Son. Love and joy will become part of the reality of your very being.

Let us start with the story of the prodigal son.[27] You know the story well, the one that tells how the young son asked for half the estate and then left home and squandered the wealth in a life of debauchery. You recall how the father waited for the return of his son, and when the son did indeed return, he celebrated because his son "was dead, and has come to life; he was lost and is found."[28] Recall how much the father loved his son no matter what the son had done. Contrast that to the older brother who had nothing but contempt and condemnation for his brother. This is the image, par excellence, of your Father's love for you. Never think that anything you could do could lessen God's love for you. His love for you is the same yesterday, today, and tomorrow. And all whom you know and love should be reassured by you of the Father's love for them. Your own love should more and more mirror that of your Father.

Let me go a little deeper into this story and share with you the nature of the love of God. The younger son had already taken half the estate, and yet the Father welcomed him back. In heaven, there is no "half of the estate"; there is only the estate. The kingdom is indivisible. You need to

---

27   Luke 15:11–32
28   Luke 15:32

know what is in store for you. You are heir to the kingdom of God. All that is in heaven will be yours. All that can be given to you by God will be given to you. Nothing more can possibly be given to you than what awaits you in heaven. This is God's generosity. When the promise is made to you that you will share in the life of God, it means that you will totally share in the life of God. See this generosity of spirit in the story of how the father treated and loved the lost son. God's generosity needs to be *felt* by you, not just accepted as a point of descriptive information about your Father.

The next point is the joy of the father in the story, the joy he had when the son returned, and how the father expressed this joy through the robe and the ring and the celebration. You must believe me when I say that God is filled with joy; joy is of the essence of the heart of God. This should rub off on you. You should be filled with joy in due course because of your relationship to God as His child. You are God's beloved child, and there is no greater love in existence than the love God has for you and each of His children. Reflective of this love and joy in God is the anger God has when people hate their neighbors or when they do harm to others. This is the same kind of anger I displayed in clearing the temple of the sellers who defiled the house of God. God seeks to bring about the fullness of love in the person and among people. Heaven has nothing of hate in it; love and joy and fullness of life are the marks of the kingdom fully realized in heaven. This kind of knowledge first enters the mind, but when you begin to realize its truth and the depth of its reality, then love and joy enter your heart through the operation of God's spirit at work in you.

Let me recall another story about my Father. It is the story of Moses on the mountain and how he encountered the burning bush.[29] God spoke to Moses from the bush, "Come no nearer. Take off your shoes, for the place on which you stand is holy ground. I am the God of your father, the God of Abraham, the God of Isaac, and the God of Jacob." Holy ground. The God of individual persons. This is what I want you to know: the holiness of God and that He is the God of individual persons.

God is *holy*. Think about what this means for a few moments. Come to know its importance. God is holy. He cannot be "unholy." His holiness is unchangeable; it is His nature. The kingdom of God is holy. This is so difficult for people to understand or even imagine because so much of life is marked by "unholiness," "unlovingness," and ugliness. None of these exist in God. God is whole, complete, lacking in nothing, all-good, all-just, and all-giving. Come to see God more and more this way. God is not vindictive. He does not sit around waiting to "catch people out" for their wrongdoing. And so it is in this time with me and this time with your Father.

Know that God is holy and that you are entering a holy time when you come to Him. You can't do anything to change His nature. Nothing you can do can unsettle Him or make Him less loving. What you can do and what you are invited and urged to do is to participate in His life and welcome the embrace He greets you with. See Him this way. Know His presence in this way. He is with you. Enter into this time with Him and me with gratitude and rejoicing. This is the heart I would give to you, a heart that responds to God's love with gratitude and rejoicing. *Who God is* should fill you and come to fill you with joy.

---

29   Exodus 3:2

Think more on the holiness of God, but this time, think in terms of goodness. Think of all the ways you have known goodness in your life. Think of the times people sacrificed their time and effort and money for you. Think of the times people set time aside especially for you. Think of the times when you had a wonderful love with certain people in your life. Think of the times when you were ill and someone nursed you back to health with a special kind of caring. Think of the times when people were so thoughtful toward others that you just knew this was the very meaning of goodness.

By contrast, think of the times when animosity, anger, jealousy, rage, revengefulness, spitefulness, or selfishness broke into relationships and tore them down or permanently damaged them. You know what the many faces of evil and what the opposite of goodness looks like. Think of God's holiness in terms of His goodness, and you will be better able to enter into this time with hope and expectancy, with love and thankfulness. This is the spirit that is right and appropriate for this time with God, your Father.

Let us recall some of the images of God that are in the psalms. These so truly tell of God and His nature and His point of view toward man. Hear these words with both your mind and heart, for you must hear God's Word with both mind and heart to better comprehend who He is and what life with Him means. This is the way you were meant to live, but evil can still come between man and God in such a way as to make His image unclear and even undesirable. Part of what this time together with God is meant to make clear is who He really is so that you might enter life more fully with Him.

The first image comes from Psalm 139: "Yahweh, you examine me and know me, you know when I am standing or sitting. It was you who created my inmost self, and put me together in my mother's womb; for all these mysteries I thank you: for the wonder of myself, for the wonder of your works. You know me through and through, from having watched my bones take shape when I was being formed in secret."[30]

Can you enter into the depth of these words? God knew you from the moment of your conception, and not just in cursory terms but in depth. He knew your soul, who you were, what you could be, what you meant to Him. He loved you then, He loves you now, and He will always love you.

You were born not just anybody. *There is no other you.* You are His beloved. He wants you to enter into this more intimate life with Him. Just as He knows you completely, He would have you know Him in intimate terms. He will reveal Himself to you more and more, and in this way, you will come to love Him.

"If Yahweh does not build the house, in vain the masons toil."[31] This is our job—to build the temple that is you. You cannot do this. You must realize that you cannot do it. This is the work of the Father and of the Word. The spirit of God is the power behind this work in making the temple complete. Have assurance in the purpose of God and in His ability to bring about His purpose in you. And His purpose is to build in you a heart that loves God and a mind that comprehends what this love is about. You must be a docile child of God. This means you must be a willing

---

30   Psalm 139:1–2; 13–15
31   Psalm 127

student of God, a willing participant in the will of God for you. Docility means that you want to be part of this life and come to that point where you know that God's will for you is perfect. To love God also includes love for His purpose, for His purpose is perfect. Let God, the master builder, be the builder of the temple of God that is you. Life cannot be better than this.

"Ah, how goodness and kindness pursue me, every day of my life; my home, the house of Yahweh, as long as I live!"[32] This is the attitude, the purest attitude of God's beloved child. Don't let your childhood of God be left at an immature level but enter fully into the household of the Lord, your home with God. This is to come to worship the God and Father of all. The more you enter into life with Him, eternal life with Him, the more this state of love for God's dwelling place will fill your soul. God will do this for you in passing on divine life to you. You yourself will come to express these words in the spontaneous worship of your heart just as the psalmist said these words from the depth of his heart. The words were not vain expressions to an unknown God but to a God known intimately. These are the words of a soul in love with God. Only God can do this in the soul of His child.

There is a part of life with God that you will come to know in your own life. "My God, my God, why have you deserted me? I call all day, my God, but you never answer. Yet, Holy One, in you our fathers put their trust, they trusted and you rescued them."[33] Know now that God is always with you, but there will come a time when He will choose to appear silent before you. This is when you must

---

32   Psalm 23:6
33   Psalm 22:1–4

know—from your own confidence and trust in Him—that He is with you, He hears your prayer, and that He is working out the best response to your cry.

Why does He do this seemingly cruel thing to you?

He is not being cruel, but He is loving you in a different way. He is building the "muscle" of your faith. Through this means, namely answering your prayer in secret, He builds your trust in Him. Over the years, you will see how wonderfully He answered all your needs, and you will become a rock of faith no matter the circumstances facing you.

When you hear my words from the cross—"My God, my God, why have you deserted me?"—know I am recalling this psalm, and I am telling my Father that I know He is with me. So too, you must come to that rock-solid faith where, no matter what happens in life, you know in the depths of your being that God is with you.

"Happy the man who never follows the advice of the wicked, or loiters on the way that sinners take, or sits about with scoffers, but finds his pleasure in the law of Yahweh. He is like a tree that is planted by water streams, yielding its fruit in season." [34]

Be planted in the soil of God. Be watered by the grace of God. Do not be "co-yoked" with those who do not know God, for they cannot lead you to Him. Rather, be co-yoked with God. Walk with Him, be with Him, and bear the fruit of His life in your life.

I am not saying you should be separate from people who are separated from God. On the contrary, you should be like a seed planted in the midst of a great garden so

---

34   Psalm 1:1–3

that you can become a plant whose beauty can be seen by all. I am saying to not be "co-yoked" with them in their purposes, which originate in separation from God. Do not be influenced by their attitudes. Do not be influenced by their politics. Do not be influenced by their understanding of the world. Do not be influenced by them, but rather become the one who influences them.

Read again the words of this psalm. Find your pleasure in the law of God, and that law is the rule of His love and life in your life. Listen to His instruction to you and take it to your heart. Let your will be formed by these words to you: "You must love the Lord your God with all your heart, with all your soul, with all your mind and with all your strength."[35] This is what it means to be "co-yoked" with God, because it is the work of God and you in the formation of your heart, mind, and spirit.

"Yahweh, I am calling, hurry to me. My prayers rise like incense, my hands like the evening offering. Yahweh, set a guard at my mouth, a watcher at the gate of my lips. Let me feel no impulse to do wrong, to share the godlessness of evildoers. To you, Yahweh, I turn my eyes. I take shelter in you, do not leave me exposed!"[36]

Come to know your nature well, for it is in your nature to have impulses that could lead you away from God. It is God who must be your protector; it is God who accepts this responsibility for you. This is what it means to be saved by God. Let Him do his work, and when you are so tempted, come to Him and seek His action to save you and to turn your thought and heart to Him. "Father, Holy One, your will be done in me as it is in heaven. Give me what I need this

35   Mark 12:29–30
36   Psalm 141:1–4; 8

day to keep me close to you, and protect me from evil."[37] This is what it means to be given all that you need by God so that you can live life fully with God each day. Protection from evil, not allowing evil to settle in the soul, having the strength to resist its temptation—this is the work of God in you. Let Him do His work in you each day. Come to your living Father each day to bring Him all your needs, including the need to be saved from the lure of evil.

God is love. In Him, there is no evil. He is the one who loves you and protects you. You are His dwelling place on earth. Come to treasure what it means to be God's beloved child each day through a special time with Him. Let me be the Word that reveals your Father more and more to you as we continue our daily walk.

---

37   Matthew 6:9-13

Chapter 5

❧

ABOUT MY MOTHER

If you look at the wedding at Cana[38] and see what my mother did, it will give you a deep insight into the love between the two of us. Her request that I do something about the lack of wine was so simple, and she trusted that I would do something. "They have no wine,"[39] was all she said to me, knowing that I would respond to the awkward and humiliating situation facing the host. Why did she believe I would do something? What did she think I would do? Without knowing what I would do and in spite of my protest that my time had not yet come, she told the servants, "Do whatever he tells you."[40]

---

38   John 2:1–12
39   John 2:3
40   John 2:5

This mustn't be seen in isolation from my life with my mother. She knew me and loved me more than anyone. She had been privy to the many instances when I was growing up and maturing as an adult when, quietly and almost without notice, I would ask my Father to help this person, heal that person, and so on. Yes, this all started early in life as a result of the life I shared with my Father. So when this situation arose at the wedding, this was no startling thing she was asking of me. She *knew* that I could help because she had seen me do it many times before. You can see that the whole affair took only a few words between us.

But there is another aspect to her request at the wedding. I responded that my time had not yet come, meaning that it was not yet time for me to begin my public ministry. The Father had not yet said the words that would begin that work. When she asked me to change the water at the wedding, I knew that such a public gesture would have a consequence in terms of public awareness of the miracle. It could not be done quietly or discreetly. My first prayer was, "Father, is now the time?" And the answer was immediate: "Yes." And so, without hesitation, I directed the servants to fill the water jars.

It is this same type of closeness to me that I would like you to have. It is the same confidence in my Father and me that I would like you to have. My mother didn't have the closeness to the Father that I had, but she had that closeness to me, which caused her to know who I was, not only as her son but as God's Son. Recall how I defined eternal life: "And eternal life is this: to know you, the only true God, and Jesus Christ whom you have sent."[41] And recall what God did for my mother when the angel told

---

41   John 17:3

her, "Mary, do not be afraid; you have won God's favor. Listen! You are to conceive and bear a son, and you must name him Jesus. He will be great and will be called Son of the Most High."[42] She always bore thankfulness in her whole being for what God had done for her, and she knew from the beginning who I was because of what the angel had told her. She knew who my Father was.

Think of this a little deeper and what it meant to her to know these things because it is the same with you. God is the unseen God, and so it was with her. She "saw" God through His actions in her and in her cousin Elizabeth. She was pregnant, just as the angel said.[43] And so was Elizabeth, just as the angel had told Zechariah. What God had told each of them had come to be, and each knew that God had done this work in them. This is why their faith in God was so strong. They believed in God before, but this action of God's made their faith impregnable. This is how it is with you too, isn't it? When you see the visible evidence of God's reality in your life, your faith should become solid as rock.

As my mother saw me grow she also saw how my relationship with my Father grew. The first time I described God as my Father was when she and Joseph found me in the temple. "Did you not know that I must be busy with my Father's affairs?"[44] She didn't understand what I meant fully at the time. She knew that God was my Father, but she didn't know the internal life I had with my Father. She wouldn't come to understand this more fully until after Pentecost, but she would come to know the nature of my prayer life more and more as time passed. She would hear me describe God as my Father repeatedly, and in the most intimate terms.

---

42   Luke 1:31–2
43   Luke 1:36
44   Luke 2:49

This is what I wish for you—that you be like my mother hearing me speak of my Father and know that God is your Father through me. Know that I will reveal the Father to you more and more just as I did with my mother.

By the time I was ready to head toward Jerusalem for the last time, my mother knew of my mission. From our many conversations together, she knew what the Father was calling me to do. This is the same knowledge you must have about my mission, because my mission is now *your* mission. Just like me, the Father calls you to a specific service to the kingdom. Like my mother, you will have an understanding of what my call was and what your call is. It is your call personally; it is what my Father will whisper to you about how you are to know, love, and serve Him. My mother's call was to be my mother and to suffer with me in my time of suffering. But it was also to care for me, to love me, to stand by me, to be faithful to me. This would be accomplished through her growing knowledge of me and the Father.

What is your relationship to my mother? Let me talk about my mother and who she should be to you. This is so important because it involves a true and proper understanding of the kingdom of God. So many today lack this understanding, and this lack hinders the proper building of the kingdom. So many have the right desire to build the kingdom but lack an essential tool in its building, and that is an understanding of what the kingdom is. When you think about the kingdom, think of it in terms of my mother for now.

The building of the kingdom of God did not begin with my life here on earth. It didn't begin with my mother's acceptance of God's plan for her. It didn't even begin with

Abraham. No, it began among individuals throughout the world who had intimations that there was a God. They didn't know Him, but God began to be revealed through intimations, dreams, thoughts, and even the stirring of modest forms of worship to an unknown God. Stirring of the consciousness among people began and developed through the ages. But God wanted a people who would be uniquely His, who would know Him in word and deed and covenant. From among all those who believed in God, God chose one person to begin this new development in the relationship between God and man. Abram, who was to become Abraham, was God's choice.[45]

And how did God do this? He asked Abram to do something. He asked him to leave his country and kin for a land God would show him. Right from the beginning, Abram acted in faith to what God asked of him. This was the new dynamic. It was the dynamic of a specific working relationship between God and man. No longer was God simply a being to believe in but a being that one should respond to with faith. And Abram's obedience to this relationship with God allowed God to carry out His plan to build a people who would be His and who would number as the stars in the sky. "Look up to heaven and count the stars if you can. Such will be your descendants."[46]

It was through the faith-filled believers of this people that the Son of Man would be made possible. They were formed through word and action. It was through my word that they were formed, and their faith was in my words, though they didn't know it. But the Word of God was preparing a people to receive the Word made flesh. When

---

45   Genesis 12
46   Genesis 15:5

Mary was born, there was already a belief that a messiah would come and that he would come through a particular family. The kingdom of God was proceeding according to the plan and method of God. Mary was formed through word and action to be my mother, and when the call came to her, she was ready and able to respond to God in faith and willingness.

But again, something new was happening here through the will of God. A "new people within a people" was being created. Mary was the first Christ-bearer, the very model of what it means to respond to the call of God in one's life. But she was a model in deeper ways than a simple response to her call. Her call was to know her son, and God His Father. In this sense, Mary was the first to enter into eternal life, the very hallmark of the kingdom. Her knowledge of God didn't begin with me. She was formed through a people who were faithful to God, who saw and knew God in word and deed. She was the fruit of a people who knew the Word of God because it had been proclaimed to them. They were faithful to the Word of God, and so they were faithful to me in that hidden form. The Trinity was at work among a people, but it had not yet made this reality visible. God was known. The Word was known, and the power of God was known. The budding kingdom of God was rooted in this people.

The kingdom of God was rooted in the souls of faithful ones, and Mary was one of these. God was always in her mind. His will was her desire. She had been formed in heart, mind, and soul through her parents who lived their faith. She was formed by her many teachers and mentors who taught her the Word and what it meant in living daily life faithful to God. She was formed by the community in which she grew up to be faithful to God and His Word and His calling. Later, when I began my mission, she continued to be a faithful servant of God. And after the resurrection and Pentecost, she continued to be what she had always been, namely a faithful servant of God. Mary was the very image of the kingdom alive in a person.

But what about today? Does Mary live? This is the proper understanding of the kingdom that needs to be known and lived. This is the part of that understanding that is deficient and that all those who would follow me need to understand deep in their souls, for it is this understanding that draws out the very meaning of the kingdom and its breadth.

The whole point of the kingdom of God is a people united in heart, mind, and soul with God. It is to begin in life on earth and continue uninterrupted into life forever united with God. What begins now in faith continues after death in intimate union with God. Life is changed to divine life in the hereafter; human life is no more. It is in this way that each person becomes changed after death through the power of God. This is your great hope on earth—that you can know God and me now, and when death arrives, you will be exactly like the good thief to whom I said, "Indeed, I promise you, today you will be with me in paradise."[47] You must take me at my word that I did this for that good man and that I do it for each of those who are in union with me. Why would one think that I couldn't bring those who are mine to be with me eternally? Why would one think I wouldn't do this? Why would one think it made any sense that I would wait to do this? I want those who are mine to be where I am and fully with my Father.[48]

47   Luke 23:39–43
48   John 14:3

When my mother died, I did the same for her. She immediately came into my presence. I was waiting for her to take her to the Father and to be among the heavenly host. And she received her crown, the very crown Paul spoke of when he said, "We do see in Jesus one who was for a short while made lower than the angels and is now crowned with glory and splendor because he submitted to death; by God's grace he had to experience death for all mankind."[49] All those who are in union with me share in the same crown of glory and splendor because they have been faithful to God and they have already been in eternal life. So my mother lives just as all those who died in union with me live now. You cannot see them, but you know that I live. And because I live, they, too, live in full vision of the Father. There should be no point of dissension among Christians on this point. Those who have gone before you already know the point of your hope. The kingdom of God lives in the living and those who have already joined me in paradise.

And so, my mother is among the heavenly host now, and what does this mean to you? It means that she continues her work in the kingdom. This is what the heavenly host does. All in heaven are in full view of God, and they fully know His will for mankind, whom they love. The love and knowledge that is in heaven is brought to bear fruit by the intercession of the saints and angels for those on earth. You do well to ask your loved ones who have gone before to pray for you and those you love, because this is what heaven is about. It is about the life of God being given to all who would seek or receive it.

My mother has a particular vantage point in the heavenly kingdom, because she knows better than all who are in heaven what I suffered and what the meaning of suffering is. She knows intimately who I am and who her Father is, and she

---

49   Hebrews 9:9

knows exactly what to ask for with utter confidence. She is my mother, but in heaven, she is the mother of the whole body of Christ. This is my Father's will. Each person who is in me, just like on earth, has a calling, a personal role to play in the building of the kingdom. This is God's calling to my mother in the heavenly kingdom, namely to take under her wing all the children of God and to love them and pray for them. Her prayers for you are powerful because she is so totally united to the will and love of God. Each of my people has his or her own role in heaven that has been assigned by my Father.

See the kingdom of God in this larger sense and understand that eternal life has no interruption but rather that the nature of that life remains the same. But in heaven, God is known totally in a life changed from human to divine. It has no end. And it is dynamic, not static, filled with love and purpose. When the world comes to an end and all is completed, then the life in heaven will not have to have a focus on earth, but the nature of the love within the kingdom will have no end. Begin to think of all those who have gone before you as being in total union with the Father and me, and through the will and power of God, they are active in praying for those on earth. See yourselves as being in union with them because of your union with me. There is no separation of persons where I am, even though you are necessarily separated from them. I am not. I am actively in union with each of them and all of them just as I am in union with you and all who are mine on earth.

Let me come to what my mother now means to you. My mother is your mother in the heavenly kingdom. This is the will of my Father, and this is my will. See what I said from the cross in the bigger picture of the total kingdom of God. I saw my mother and the disciple I loved standing there, and I said to my mother, "Woman, this is your son." Then I said to John, "This is your mother."[50] It was understood by all who came to hear this from my mother and John that she was the mother of all the disciples while she lived, and later, this would be understood as the meaning in terms of eternal life and the kingdom of God.

See this woman I loved so dearly on earth and love so completely in heaven as your spiritual mother. You *are* the disciple I love. This is the nature of the kingdom of God. She is so totally united with the Father and me that she can respond to intercede for you within the grace of her own calling. Through the grace my Father has given her and through me, she will hear your prayers and become intimately involved in your life as your heavenly mother. Come to love her as your spiritual mother. I wish this to be so. Enter into this fuller meaning and dynamic of the kingdom of God and invite others to do so as well.

---

50   John 19:26–7

Chapter 6

～

ABOUT YOU

We are halfway through our walk together, and this intimate time should give you hope that this relationship can be a model of an ongoing walk that can last the rest of your life. Even at this point, can you think of anything in life that could be more wonderful than a daily intimate time with your God, friend, Lord, and savior? As we continue, I want to talk about you and who you are to me and my Father and to tell you that we need you.

Imagine that for a few moments: The God and creator of the universe needs you. Let that truth sink into your very soul. Just as you need God, God needs you. He made you to share in His life, but He also needs you to spread His life to others. Without you and millions like you, God's work on earth cannot be done. Remember what I asked, "But when the Son of Man comes, will he find any faith on earth?"[51] God has placed much in the hands of man, in the will of man, and in the desire of man for God. On so fragile a base has God seen fit to build the kingdom of God. When you think about it, how else would God have gone about building the kingdom? What good would it have done if God had chosen a method to build the kingdom that didn't involve the changing of the human heart? How could God be a true savior of man without saving the human heart from itself?

And this applies to you, dear one, who has chosen me as your own. This is why it is more important than anything else to tell you how much you mean to God. I have said it before during this walk that you and all of mankind were the reason for creation so that all might share in the eternal life of God. Man separated himself from God and continues to do so to this day through his own nature, will, and actions. God must be the way to overcome man's innate tendency to stray, even when man has made the decision to follow me and be faithful to God. Think how difficult it is for man to come to God when he has every reason not to. "How hard it is for those who have riches to enter the kingdom of God! How hard it is to enter the kingdom of God. It is easier for a camel to pass through the eye of a needle than for a rich man to enter the kingdom of God."[52]

But you have decided to enter the kingdom of God, and how wonderful for you and others that you have decided to do so. Now I have these words for you to indicate what this

51   Luke 18:8
52   Mark 10:25. "Eye of a needle" denotes a small entry way designed to let people in but keep camels out.

life means to you now and forevermore. I want to break open some scripture meant to deepen your life with me and with your Father in heaven. Hear me as I speak to you with love, the very love of God.

Before any mission I might give you, before any specific call to use your talents and gifts, before any part you might play in the building of the kingdom, you must realize that *you* are God's beloved. It is you He wishes to share His life with. My Father and I are one, and I will be the way for you to share our life. It is I, your constant companion, who will bring you to the Father, and it is I who will share His love for you. When you are with me and in me, you enter the very bosom of God. You cannot get closer to God than you can through me. I am the way, the truth, and the life.[53] In each of these ways, I will bring you into the heart of God. This is the first and primary task I have as Lord and savior and the way the kingdom of God is built, one "living stone"[54] at a time. The very purpose of God lies in His desire that you be in complete union with Him. This is the very meaning of holiness, and this is the goal of our companionship. Do not think of tasks to be done or objectives to be accomplished. The total immersion of your soul in God is God's purpose.

Recall my baptism. Hear the words my Father said to me, "You are my Son, the beloved; my favor rests on you."[55] He said these words to you at your baptism when you were inserted into the very life of the Trinity. This was real

---

53   John 14:6
54   1 Peter 2:4–5. He is the living stone, rejected by men but chosen by God and precious to him; set yourselves close to him so that you too, the holy priesthood that offers the spiritual sacrifices which Jesus Christ has made acceptable to God, may be living stones making a spiritual house.
55   Luke 3:21–2

water, real spirit. Unless a man is born through water and the spirit, he cannot enter the kingdom of God.[56] You are already in the kingdom through your baptism, but you must enter it in spirit and truth.[57] It is this spirit and this truth that I speak of now—your spirit and the truth of your very being.

Have no gods beside me.[58] Do not let other things or people or ambitions replace me on the throne of your heart. I cannot be your Lord if you allow another master to rule you. You must examine yourself scrupulously to determine if something else is lord of your life.

Here is a way to do this task: Ask yourself what motivates you when you get up in the morning. To whom do you effectively make your morning offering? Is it to God, or is it to busyness, greed, power, money, entertainment, or sloth? Are you looking to do God's will each day? Have you discovered that God's will is the source of your very happiness? Do you long to do His will? If not, then you need to seek this level of intimacy with me, for God's will is your very food and strength. Do you believe me in this?

Sit with me quietly for a few moments and tell me what you want in life. Tell me the true desire of your heart. Then we can go from there.

Here is my desire for you. I want you to come to me each day for a set period of time. This is our time together, and this is the time I can do great things in you, even when you are unaware of what I am doing. Know that my desire is to be with you, to share eternal life with you, to create

---

56   John 3:5
57   John 4:24. God is spirit, and those who worship must worship in spirit and truth.
58   Deuteronomy 5:7

a new heart in you. I shall give you a new heart and put a new spirit in you; I shall remove the heart of stone from your body and give you a heart of flesh instead.[59] You will not notice this transformation from day to day, but over time, you will see that you are being changed. God's "heart of flesh" is to be your heart too. This is the essential work of God in you.

Let us look into the heart of God to see what it is like. This is the image for your own heart, and what the "remake of your heart" will look like more and more as you spend time with me. The heart of God is the essential image of the kingdom of God.

"God is light, there is no darkness in Him at all."[60] In my hour of darkness, when darkness ruled,[61] God's heart was full of light, and so was mine. Even when darkness prevails around you, your heart can be filled with light. There is nothing on earth that can bring darkness into the heart of God. He is blinded by nothing. He is fooled by nothing. He is bewitched by nothing. He cannot be led astray. The more your heart is filled with light, the more you will be unassailable by outside influences or powers. "For it is not against human enemies that we have to struggle, but against Sovereignties and the Powers who originate the darkness in this world, the spiritual army of evil in the heavens."[62] Believe in the reality of evil that is the cause of darkness in the world, and believe in the light of God that overcomes the darkness. There is no darkness that can overcome God. So, in your own heart, should darkness exist, be not afraid, because God has you in the

---

59 Ezekiel 36:26–7
60 1 John 1:5
61 Luke 22:53
62 Ephesians 6:12

palm of His hand,[63] and it is his light that overcomes the darkness. Darkness cannot overcome or deceive you when you are God's. And you *are* God's.

In heaven, there is no darkness or falsehood at all. No lie or falsehood can live in the kingdom of God without being uncovered and destroyed. Falsehood is from the evil one. It must be guarded against as an enemy of God, for it finally leads away from God. The light of God exposes falsehood and destroys it. You can count on me to expose any falsehood in your soul, for it must be destroyed as God's enemy. People don't realize how destructive falsehood is in their lives. How can trust be built when falsehood or deceit lies beneath, hidden from view? And what is the very purpose of falsehood except to gain some advantage over another? Think about what falsehood has done to relationships in your own life experience.

God cannot be deceived. There is no game playing with God. Look at what happened to Ananias and Sapphira when they tried to deceive the community by trying to keep part of the proceeds in the sale of a property. Each died because of their deceit.[64] Look at what acts of dishonesty and falsehood have done in today's world. Falsehood is never from God, and falsehood cannot be tolerated by God or the kingdom of God. If there is falsehood in you, God will take action to remove it from your soul so that you may live fully eternal life. This is because falsehood undermines the kingdom of God. If you have falsehood within you, and most people do, welcome God's cleansing of your soul. Welcome this as you would a surgeon operating on a cancer.

---

63   Isaiah 49:16
64   Acts 5:1–5

Part of the change of the heart, as you can see, comes from purifying the heart of things that operate against God's love. Cultivate that prayer that asks God to uncover these things and to create the understanding and will to rid yourself of whatever is tempting you. Do this for your sake and for the sake of God and His work in you. "Save us from the evil one."[65] Do not think of this so much as evil that lives outside you but as the evil that may have settled in your soul. This is the work of God, namely to cleanse your soul of such things so that you may be God's work of art in all the glory He had in mind for you from the beginning. You are God's work of art, and there is no beauty like the soul purified from the dross that can come into the human soul. Welcome the purity of the heart of God and ask Him to transform you more into his image.

In coming close to God, you must first take those steps that are needed to break from those things that lead away from God. Eternal life is about entering more fully into that very life that is in God. Clearing away impediments is equivalent to opening the door to the heart from the inside.[66] In effect, this is giving God permission to be the guest in your soul that will transform you more into His image in heart, mind, and spirit.

Recall the story of the woman at the well.[67] Recall that part of the story when I told her of her real life and her five husbands, and remember how I told her that the one with whom she was now living wasn't her husband.[68] This is equivalent to what I have been describing above. I told her

---

65   Matthew 6:13
66   Revelations 3:20. "Look, I am standing at the door, knocking."
67   John 4:5–42
68   John 4:17-18

the true state of her being in terms of how she had lived and was living. This is what I will do for you. But the point isn't to condemn or induce guilt but to clarify what the reality is in terms of the state of one's soul and the impact on relationship with God. The next thing that I told her was what worship looked like. In effect, I was telling her what life with God looked like. I said to her, "You worship what you don't know; we worship what we do know; for salvation comes from the Jews. But the hour will come—in fact, it is here already—when the worshippers will worship the Father in spirit and in truth."[69] This is where I wish to lead you, namely, to worshipping the Father in spirit and truth.

Let me begin this way. The woman at the well, because I told her who she was, believed that I am the Messiah. As we continue our walk, I will tell you who you are too. This is part of the method of God, and this is part of the personal revelation that comes from walking with me. Just as it was with the woman at the well, I will tell you who you are in a way that reveals who I am. From what I told her, she moved to thoughts of the Messiah, and then I confirmed that I was the one: "I who am speaking to you, I am he."[70] You will come to know beyond doubt that I, who am with you each day, am the Messiah of God, the Word of God, the revealer of God to the human soul.

In this you will begin to experience joy that comes from me, and that peace that no man can take from you. "Peace be with you."[71] And I will go further. Just as I did with Thomas, I will tell you to "put your finger in my side and in my hands," and you will have the same response as him, "My Lord and my God."[72] Just as Peter knew who I

---

69   John 4:22-23
70   John 4:26
71   John 20:21
72   John 20:27-29

was by the working of the Holy Spirit, so too will you come to know beyond doubt who I am and what I am doing. No person or thing can give this gift to you. It is the gift of knowledge that comes from God alone. And, like the two on the road to Emmaus, your heart will burn within you.[73] This is our walk "to Emmaus."

And now recall my appearance to Mary Magdalene after the resurrection.[74] This story does not stand in isolation from her life with me after she became a disciple. More than any other disciple, except my mother and Peter, Mary loved me the most. In her heart, she had such deep thankfulness for what I had freed her from,[75] but even more than this, she had seen how I had healed and freed others from similar evils. She herself had become such a help to those who were oppressed by evil in their lives, and she helped bring many to me so that I might save them as well. She had come to know me over the course of her travels with the apostolic group, and she had also come to love me deeply. That is why on that Sunday morning her instinct was to reach out to me and hold me because her joy was so overwhelming when she realized it was I speaking to her.

And so it will be with you as time passes and we continue our daily time together. You and I will become more one in spirit and truth. You will become that changed heart who truly loves God. It will be no act, no useless action purporting to be the real thing. Your heart will truly belong to God, and you will love Him with all your heart, with all your soul, and with all your strength.[76] This will

---

73   Luke 24:32
74   John 20:11-18
75   Luke 8:2
76   Deuteronomy 6:5

not come from any action of yours, except to cooperate with my grace, but rather it will come from the unseen presence and action of God in your soul. This is what happened to the woman at the well; God came into her very being and stirred her love for Him and for me. This is the essential work of God, and it is this very work that creates the kingdom of God on earth.

Let us recall again the wedding feast at Cana.[77] Can you imagine a feast without food or wine? What kind of celebration would that be? What would you think of the host who failed to provide the basic ingredients for a celebration feast? But recall what was said of me: "This was the first of the signs given by Jesus: it was at Cana in Galilee. He let his glory be seen, and his disciples believed in him."[78] This is what I went on to do repeatedly throughout my earthly mission. I showed the presence and action of God among the people. I showed the love of God for the people and for individual persons. I showed the way that I am with people, namely through visible actions that touch people, through healing and freeing, through stories that tell of God, through stories that reveal who people are to God, through the Word that touches the very soul of man.

And so with you, dear one, temple of God, you are God's own child. You are His beloved, and I am with you as the one who reveals Him to you. I am the one who will work out that greatest miracle of all—love for God in the depths of your very being.

---

77   John 2:1-12
78   John 2:11

Chapter 7

COME AND SEE

Just as I invited Andrew and another disciple to "come and see" when they asked me where I lived,[79] so too it is with you now as we continue our time together. Just as spending time with me meant so much to those two ("we have found the Messiah"), so too does this time mean much to you. But I was new to them. They were followers of John, who proclaimed to them when he saw me, "Look, there is the lamb of God."[80] It was this proclamation that led them to investigate me for themselves. But for you who know who I am, the "come and see" invitation is so that I can reveal more about who I am and, because my Father and I are one, who my Father is as well. So enter into a quiet time now to be alone with me so that I may speak to your soul.

---

79   John 1:35–41
80   John 1:29

The love of God is like a dragnet cast into the sea, one that brings in hauls of all kinds. When it is full, the fishermen haul it ashore. When they sit down, they collect the good ones in a basket and throw away those that are of no use. This is how it will be at the end of time; the angels will appear and separate the wicked from the just and then throw the wicked into the blazing furnace where there will be weeping and grinding of teeth.[81] Do not think of this as a threat, but rather think of this in terms of God weeping over those who will be lost. He leaves in the hands of each person the choice to enter into life with Him.

Do not think that God is an unjust God, for He knows those who would have entered into life with Him if they'd had a chance. He takes this into account. But there are those who reject Him. This is the truth. The soul does not die, and the soul does not lose its ability to think and realize what is going on. Those who are not with God or saved from eternal separation from Him because of His loving justice will be eternally separated from Him. And this will be an eternal torment to them similar to the grief one experiences when a deep tragedy happens to him or her. The image of hellfire conveys the level of torment they will experience eternally, and part of this will come from knowing they can do nothing about it. This is the despair of eternal separation from God.

What does this have to do with "come and see?" You shall enter into the very love of God during this time with me, and then your soul will shrivel at the very thought of separation from Him even for a moment. Your prayer will be, "Lord, never let me be parted from you," because the love of God will so capture your soul. Even now, as

---

81   Matthew 13:47–50

we are together, the love of God is coming into your very being. You may not even sense it, but over time, you will mysteriously discover that you love God more than you ever have. This is the unseen working of God in your soul.

It is this experience of the love of God for you and your own love for God that will reveal what it means to be separated from God, and this will create in your heart and spirit a horror at the thought of ever being separated from God both now or at any time in the future. This is part of the heart that is living in eternal life. And you will then know why God, in his mercy and love, wants everyone to know that they can be part of His life and that they can also be separate from eternal life. There is a longing in the heart of those in love with God that those separated from God not be left out of the heavenly banquet.

Hear me, feel my presence, sense my being here with you. When you hear these words I speak to you, you know that it is I who am here with you, and you know deep within your being that the words I speak are truth.

You know I am here and that you are with God, Father, Son, and Holy Spirit. When I say, "Come and see," it is to our presence I bring you. This is the awareness I want you to have each day. Come to me each day and hear what I have to say to you, be aware of my presence, and know within the depths of your being that divine love has come to you, of which human love is but an image.

Recall the story of the widow of Nain.[82] "Now soon afterward he went to a town called Nain, accompanied by a great number of people. When he was near the gate of the town it happened that a dead man was being carried out for burial, the only son of his mother, and she was a

82   Luke 7:11–17

widow." Twice now in her life, tragedy had come to this woman, first with the early death of her husband and now with the death of her son. What would she do to support herself? What would she do in her loneliness? She wanted to die. Her misery and grief and concern were so deep.

"When the Lord saw her he felt sorry for her. 'Do not cry,' he said. Then he went up and put his hand on the bier and the bearers stood still, and he said, 'Young man, I tell you to get up.' And the dead man sat up and began to talk, and Jesus gave him to his mother." Can you imagine the joy this grieving mother felt when she saw that her son was alive? Can you imagine the amazement of the crowd when they saw what had happened?

Do you think even greater things than this are impossible for God? Do you think this was but an isolated instance of the compassion God has for a person? You must come to know that my love for you is equal to the love I had for this woman. When sorrow or fear or foreboding comes to you, you must know that I am with you through it all, that I am never separated from you. The will of the Father is in me for you. I know what He wants for you, and I know how to bring it about. Do not think that my hand is shortened so that I cannot save.[83] I am the same yesterday, today and tomorrow.[84] Have this confidence that I am your savior and Lord.

There is nothing that I cannot do to bring about the will of God in you. No matter what your situation today, no matter what has happened to you in the past that may have injured you, no matter what happens to you tomorrow, know that all these have my mark on them, that past, present, and future are within my mandate for you. All that hinders

---

83   Isaiah 50:2
84   Hebrews 13:8

your life with God is the subject of my mandate, and all that could provide a stumbling block in the future is the subject of my care. Know that the one who raised the young man from the dead and returned him to his mother can do all that is required to bring you the fullness of eternal life.

Stop for a moment now and receive my assurance deep in your heart and soul. Take some time to know that this is the love of God at work in you. Never be afraid, for it is God's will that I keep you safe from anything that could threaten your eternal life. Know that I mean to bring about the fullness of eternal life in you. You will know the love of God *from within the very heart of God, my heart.*

There are two aspects of the story of the dead man restored to life that relate to you. The first is that I am concerned about life and eternal life in the present. This is why I brought the man back to life, because it had to do with the mother's life now. Know that every day is important to you and me because eternal life is in the here and now. *What happens in your life is under my care.* It is now that the heart is formed, and it is now that the seed of the Word is dropped in to the heart and mind to bear fruit at a later date. Seeds that were dropped in before are being brought to bear fruit now.

The second is that everything in eternal life brings glory to God. The glory of God is man fully alive. This is what I have come to give and what God gives, namely abundant life. I have come so that they may have life and have it to the full.[85] The raising of the man brought glory to God. The happiness and joy of the widow brought glory to God. Abundant life in you brings glory to God. Do not think of this in material terms, although all material aspects of your life are within my care when I am the Lord

---

85   John 10:10

of your life. Think of it rather as the state of your heart and mind and spirit. It is a state of peace and happiness in your soul. Have that thought within you that all is well, that all is within God's view and care, and that all is within God's loving purpose. Sit with these thoughts for a few moments and let them enter your heart.

Imagine yourself with me at the table at the Last Supper, and with all that you now know, hear these words of mine spoken to you personally. If anyone loves me, that man will keep my word, and my Father and I will love him. And we will come to him and make our home in him. Peace I bequeath to you, my own peace I give you.[86] Feel this peace permeate you. *Let* it permeate you. It is my gift to you. Receive it with thanksgiving. Do not let your heart be troubled or afraid.[87] With me, there is no need to fear or be afraid. The moment you feel fear, come to me, and I shall give you peace anew. Know with whom you are living your life, and do not be afraid. Know that I am with you always—all the way to the end of time.[88] How can I lie to you? How could I deceive you in this? I cannot. Know what I say is true in the depths of your being. Stand on this solid ground.

Make your home in me as I make mine in you. I am the vine, and you are the branch. You are to bear much fruit for me. It is to the glory of my Father that you should bear much fruit.[89] Your transformed heart and spirit will bear fruit to those around you. God's life in you cannot be contained; it must love others in turn. The fruit that you will bear is the fruit of the love between you and the

---

86   John 14:23, 27
87   John 14:27
88   Matthew 28:20
89   John 15:4–5, 8

Father and between you and me. It will not be something you even have to think about. It will come about naturally because of your life with me.

Be aware of others and their needs. When you come to me each day, ask me to help you serve others, to help you be aware of others around you and their needs. Like me, your loving heart will desire what is best for them. You did not choose me. No, I chose you, and I commission you to go out and bear fruit, fruit that will last.[90] Love all who are in your life, even those who seem estranged from you. Think of yourself as a garden that is seeded by me, and each of these seeds is meant for someone. Let your garden bloom so that those who are to be recipients of those blooms may receive them.

You must make sure that the ground is tilled and fertile. This is up to you. It is your part in the work of the two of us—co-yoked in the work of God. It is mine to plant seed that will bear fruit in you. It is the two together, the fertile soil of your soul and the fruit-bearing seed I plant. The soil of your soul is kept fertile through these daily meetings with me. Try to see these times as the most important times for the development of your soul, benefiting you and all those in your life. God always brings about these two benefits: your soul and the souls around you.

Do not think you have to accomplish the work in others, for that is my job and the job of my Father. My Father draws people to me, and I respond to their call. You cannot do this, but what you do is vitally important in this work. It is in you that people see the image of me. This is the primary fruit you bear. Do you see how important this time with me is, because it is through this time with me that you allow

90   John 15:16–7

me to transform you into my image? For those with eyes to see and ears to hear, that image is compelling to the soul. Do not think you have to teach or preach, although I may call you to either of these from time to time. But teaching and preaching is not your primary call. Your primary call is to have me formed in your soul more and more through time so that others may see me in you. This is the primary witness to eternal life that you give. Do you see that you can do this? Do you pray for the desire to be this? That desire should fill your heart and spirit over time.

Hear these words of mine: Father, the hour has come. Glorify your Son so that the Son may glorify you; and through the power over all mankind that you have given him, let him give eternal life to all those you have entrusted to him. And eternal life is this: to know you, the only true God, and Jesus Christ, whom you have sent. Holy Father, keep those you have given me true to your name so that they may be like us. I am not asking you to remove them from the world but to protect them from the evil one. They do not belong to the world any more than I belong to the world. Consecrate them in the truth; your word is truth. Father, may they be one in us, as you are in me and I am in you, so that the world may believe it was you who sent me. I have made your name known to them and will continue to make it known so that the love with which you loved me may be in them and so that I may be in them.[91]

Yes, hear these words again and again so that they may seep into your soul: my Father in me, I in him, and you in us. This is eternal life. It is a life shared between the three of us. See this as the fundamental work of God in each soul who would be His. It is not a following of laws and rules but a following of the heart toward God. It is a matter

---

91   John 17:1–3, 11, 15–7, 21, 26

of the heart, mind, soul, and spirit. It includes every aspect of the person and brings the dignity of man to its fullest realization. It is man fully alive in God.

To you, beloved one, God gives His life and calls you into the very life of the Trinity. This is all about you and the life you have with God. Come and see how our life together grows from simply being together each day.

Chapter 8

⁓

RISEN LIFE

"**N**ow if Christ raised from the dead is what has been preached, how can some of you be saying that there is no resurrection from the dead? If there is no resurrection of the dead, Christ himself cannot have been raised, and if Christ has not been raised then our preaching is useless and your believing is useless; indeed, we are shown up as witnesses who have committed perjury before God, because we swore in evidence before God that he raised Christ to life. For if the dead are not raised, Christ has not been raised, and if Christ has not been raised, you are still in your sins. And what is more serious, all who have died in Christ have perished. If our hope in Christ has been for this life only, we are the most unfortunate of people."[92]

---

92   1 Corinthians 15:12–19

I am the risen one, the firstborn from the dead. Eternal life is in God, and I have come to bring man into eternal life in the here and now. However, when the time comes, each shall be raised to new life in a new and imperishable body just as my Father raised me to this new life in an imperishable body. Risen life marks the change from human life to divine life. It marks the movement from the way divine life interacts with human life now and the way human life is transformed by God into divine life in the hereafter.

It is through the Holy Spirit at work in the human soul that one comes into God's presence and through whom God takes up His home in a person. This is the life I brought to man. Before me, God had not acted in quite the same way. *Through* the prophets, God had acted to make His word known, but the *spirit* did not *dwell within* the prophet. The person as the dwelling place of God, the temple of God's presence, is often taken for granted in these days, but this only became possible through me and my sacrifice. It was my work on earth to make the *indwelling* of God possible for mankind. "Unless I go, the Advocate will not come to you; and if I go, I will send him to you."[93]

In effect, the divine was taking up abode within the human soul. This was the new life I brought to mankind. This was the bridging of what had been lost to mankind. Until now, belief in God was an external thing, something believed because of an event or words spoken by someone else. It was not something that was internal, that came from the indwelling of God. Many in the church today could enter this life by a simple decision to do so but remain, in

---

93   John 16:7

effect, outside this new life I brought to mankind. That is why the faith level of many, even though baptized, is at such a low level and their "witness" is such a scandal to those who might otherwise seek me.

Remember the story of the foolish bridesmaids who said to the bridegroom, "Lord, Lord, open the door for us." But He replied, "I tell you solemnly, I do not know you."[94] It is the divine life in each person that the Father and I see. Communion with God is the issue. This is the life I brought, and it is the life offered by God to all those who would enter. It is not the offering of "holocaust or sacrifice"[95] that God wants; it is not simple belief in God that God wants. That is not why I came and died and rose again. It is the risen life I came to give, and that is the life of total communion with God. And this involves the offering of one's life, as I offered mine. I solemnly tell you that unless a wheat grain falls on the ground and dies, it remains a single grain, but if it dies, it yields a rich harvest.[96] This is not a superficial life. Risen life means the death of the old self, which is replaced by the new man through God.[97] Risen life is a new creation, a new state of soul, and a new entry into divine life. Divine life recreates what is human. This process is the beginning of the move from what is human and finite to something divine and everlasting. There is shallowness about these matters today that creates massive confusion about what God is about, what I am about, and what each person is called to be. Let there be no ambiguity about life with God and what it is

94   Matthew 25:12
95   Mark 12:33
96   John 12:24
97   2 Corinthians 5:17. "And for anyone who is in Christ, there is a new creation; the old creation has gone, and now the new one is here. It is all God's work."

that God wants. Remember what I said to those who are lukewarm: "I know all about you—how you are neither cold nor hot. I wish you were one or the other, but since you are neither, but only lukewarm, I will spit you out of my mouth."[98]

Again, I told my followers what lay ahead of me when I was heading to Jerusalem. "And he began to teach them that the Son of Man was destined to suffer grievously, to be rejected by the elders and the chief priests and the scribes, and be put to death, and after three days to rise again, and he said all this quite openly."[99] What if I had told my Father, "I don't like your plan"? What would have become of mankind? But I knew my Father's mind and will, and I was one with Him in it. To those who heard me say this, they either couldn't understand it at all or they dismissed it as nonsense. Even Peter tried to dissuade me. "Peter started to remonstrate with him. But turning and seeing his disciples, he rebuked Peter and said to him, 'Get behind me, Satan! Because the way you think is not God's way but man's.'"[100]

It is the same today. People do not know the will of the Father in terms of eternal life, and view it in the most simplistic terms. They believe that simple belief is enough or that being good in life is enough. They think, "God is just, so how could He condemn anyone who has lived a good life or has believed in God?" But I say to you now, as I said to all then, it is not those who say to me, "Lord, Lord," who will enter the kingdom of heaven but the person who does the will of my Father in heaven. When the day comes, many will say to me, "Lord, Lord, did

---

98   Revelations 3:15–6
99   Mark 8:31–2
100   Mark 8:33

we not prophesy in your name, cast out demons in your name, work many miracles in your name?" Then I shall tell them to their faces, "I have never known you; away from me, you evil men!"[101]

Is this distinction clear to you? Many people believe in God but are not connected to the real God in any way. It has always been so. Before I came, there were multitudes who believed in a god but were never connected in any way to God. God showed Himself to certain people to reveal who He is and to begin a process whereby people might be united with Him. But until I came to make intimate life with God possible, eternal life was really unknown to man. You have the privilege of entering into the fruit I bore for God; it is you and all like you who would enter into daily communion with God that I came for. This is why I said, "Enter by the narrow gate, since the road that leads to perdition is wide and spacious, and many take it; but it is the narrow gate and a hard road that leads to life, and only a few take it."[102]

The life I offer you now is this narrow way. Many are afraid to take this narrow way for fear of what God may ask of them. Will God ask of you what He asked of me? If so, why would anyone choose that path for him or herself? But I say to you that God has His perfect plan for you. You are completely in His mind, and His will for you is perfect. It is the holy way, the wonder-filled way, the way that will bear much fruit through you. Enter into this life with God day-by-day. Come close to God each day. Know the love of God each day for yourself and for all those in your life. Let Him lead you in His way, and you will know

---

101   Matthew 7:21–3
102   Matthew 7:13–4

the fullness of eternal life in this world. But know that it is the narrow way, and few enter. There is a sadness you yourself will come to know, a sadness that is in the heart of God for man, knowing that so few choose Him over other paths that can be followed in life. If only they knew the cost of this choice.

Let me now turn to my risen life and my return to the Father. Let me describe the nature of heaven as I know it and as all who have entered into it and who have gone before you know it. Know what it means when the Father says to you, "Well done, good and faithful servant; come and join in your master's happiness."[103] There is a twofold hope: the hope that is now in your life with God and the hope of everlasting life with Him when this life is ended. Have both hopes in you so that you know what God has in mind for you both now and forevermore. I speak now of the afterlife toward which all current life moves.

"On this mountain, Yahweh Sabaoth will prepare for all peoples a banquet of rich food, a banquet of fine wines. He will remove the mourning veil covering all peoples, and the shroud enwrapping all nations, he will destroy death forever. The Lord Yahweh will wipe away the tears from every cheek. That day it will be said: See, this is our God in whom we hoped for salvation."[104] Yes, it is a life without tears or mourning. It is a life where all therein, no matter their ethnic or national origin, are one in spirit, one in full view of God. There is a happiness that is described as a banquet, a celebration that is filled with love and knowledge. Heaven can never end, and it is filled with life and vigor.

---

103   Matthew 25:21
104   Isaiah 25:6–9

It is the nature of this life and vigor that in many ways mirrors what the life of grace produces on earth. The action of God in one's life on earth frees the person to become more of who he or she is. Spiritual and emotional barriers, like pride, cowardice and sloth, are overcome. Insight into the wonder of life and its meaning is given. And this increases awareness of God and man. When one comes into the full presence of God, all hindrances to the life of grace disappear, the person is totally whom he or she is and was meant to be at conception. The soul is filled with love, and the love of God radiates totally through the person.

St. Térèse of Lisieux, the little flower, said that she would spend her time in heaven doing good on earth. The saints in heaven are freed from the human limitations of doing good for others in the sense that they are totally free to love others and to be solicitous toward others in their prayer. And more than that, they have come to know the mind of God in ways unimaginable on earth. So your loved ones who have gone into the heavenly kingdom do indeed pray for you. They are aware of your needs, and they have been given the power to intercede in prayer on your behalf. And they become aware when prayers are answered, and the rejoicing in heaven because of this is beyond any earthly comparison.

When I told the "good thief" that he would be with me in paradise that very day,[105] he wasn't going to enter some inert bliss but a state of unending joy and active involvement in the process of grace. He would become a source of prayer for those he loved on earth and others who would be brought to his attention. This is so for all

---

105   Luke 23:43

the saints. The preeminent example of this life is my mother. Picture her as a totally transparent channel of grace for others. This is the image of heaven you should have of those you love who have gone on before you, and you should ask them to pray for you. You should ask your heavenly mother to pray for you. You should ask me to act for you. This is the correct picture of the abundance of grace that is active in heaven. And God is at the center of it all. When life on earth finally comes to an end and when I have brought all those who are mine with me into the heavenly kingdom, there will be no further need for prayer for those on earth. At that time, the life of grace in heaven will have changed focus to one of unending enjoyment of the gifts of all who are there.

Worship in heaven is spontaneous and natural. It comes out of the love that is pervasive in the soul of one who sees God. It does not have to be "acted" or manufactured. It is totally real. Even as those souls on earth who are in love with God come to have joy in their very being, so too is the joy of heaven. The joy is complete. Love of neighbor is complete. Love of God is total. When it is said there will be no more tears, this is such an understatement. It is the joy of heaven: joy at the sight of God and knowledge of who He is, joy at coming to know all the saints, joy at seeing the giftedness of the human soul. This giftedness is shared totally with God and the others.

Think of the happiness that human giftedness brings on earth and then try to imagine what this giftedness would be like when freed of all earthly limitation. The spirit of those in heaven is that of total giving which yields the unhindered giving of each one's giftedness. This is man fully alive, and the glory of God is man fully alive.

This is the truth of heaven. And it is why God created man. I came to give abundant life[106] on earth in the soul united to God, and the abundance of this life reaches its perfection in heaven.

Let me come at this from a different perspective. Why would those on earth assume that those who have gone before wouldn't want to pray for their loved ones and others on earth? Doesn't that seem as natural as night following day? This is the very nature of love—to be concerned about those loved and to want to help those loved. And love is perfected in heaven. The needs of those on earth are made known to those in heaven through me, through my knowledge of the need of each. And the prayers of those in heaven are answered through me by the will of the Father. See these as the wonder of God's plan of salvation, as the totally life-giving nature of eternal life. Feel the joy of this vision of life with God.

Let me give you the image of the heavenly Eucharist. In referring to the Eucharist, recall how I told the disciples to "do this as a memorial of me."[107] At that time, I also said that I would not eat it again until it was fulfilled in the kingdom of God.[108] The Eucharist on earth is a foretaste of the heavenly Eucharist, except "doing this in memory of me" is no longer necessary. The heavenly host is gathered around me, and I am completely given to each person. Their transformation is complete, and they fully become channels of my life to one another. There is no need for further transformation. This process of transformation unleashes the greatest worship of God in love and awe one could imagine, and even more.

106	John 10:10
107	Luke 22:19
108	Luke 22:16

This is the image of the heavenly Eucharist I'd like you to have. Think of the richest choirs on earth giving praise to God and then try to translate this into an image of the heavenly host, with heavenly giftedness, praising and worshipping God. It is a scene of total love and joy and fulfillment. The prayer is no longer the sacrifice of praise but praise that comes from knowing God totally, seeing His glory, and worshipping out of an abundance of love and joy that fills one's being.

Never think of heaven as a static or boring place. This is so foreign to the reality of heaven. Just think of what life with the Father and me is like on earth in those times when you have experienced the goodness of God. If God is like this on earth, how could it possibly be that God suddenly becomes inactive in heaven? Even a moment's thought should dispel such a notion. Even now as you pray your way through these words, you should rejoice at the very thought of heaven and the promise it holds for you. When you have those moments of vivid awareness of the glory of God, think then about what the total view of God must mean. Think what this risen life in all its fullness must mean. Think of the glory of God made manifest through man fully alive. And think, too, that this was God's purpose in creating man.

This is risen life, eternal life. You see it dimly now,[109] but then you will see God face-to-face, and you will know the glory of creation.

---

109   1 Corinthians 13:12. "Now we are seeing a dim reflection in a mirror; but then we shall see face-to-face. The knowledge that I have now is imperfect; but then I shall know as fully as I am known."

Chapter 9

❧

THE MISSION

All authority in heaven and on earth has been given to me. Go, therefore, make disciples of all the nations. Baptize them in the name of the Father, and of the Son, and of the Holy Spirit. Teach them to observe all the commands I gave you. And know that I am with you always—yes, to the end of time.[110] Yes, this is the fundamental mission of my followers on earth until the end of time, and you have your part in it. But it is important to know what this means.

Reflect back on God's purpose in creating man. God created man to fully share in His life. And because of the state of man's separation from God, I came to make that

---

110   Matthew 28:18–20

full union with God possible. I am the gateway to that full life with God. God did not intend that this life be the preserve of a few but would become the life of the world in due course. This is the vision of God, and it was my mission to make this possible. And it is the mission of the church forevermore to make this possible. But what does it mean to "baptize all nations in the name of the Father, and of the Son, and of the Holy Spirit?"

This walk with you has described a life made available through me, with me, and in me. The life of the Father is made available to all who are in me. It is real fullness of life in God and from God, and it is to be an everlasting life in complete union with God. This is not a life of tokenism or shallow belief. It is the life of authentic faith that brings about the kingdom of God on earth. It is a holy life and a life of giving and sharing what one has with others. It is a life of transformation that also transforms life on earth into something that is God-centered and that bears good fruit for all on earth. It is life built on the love of God for man.

To baptize in the name of the Father, and of the Son and of the Holy Spirit means to bring the nations of the world into the internal life of God so that the life of God, Father, Son, and Holy Spirit permeates all of the life of the nation. This process transforms life into a ferment that seeks to bring the love and understanding of God to all. This is not a simple mission or process.

The ideal is not simple belief in God but life with, in, and through God. It is through the power of God that this life is possible, not through the efforts of man, although man must choose to enter this life and to cooperate with God in its formation. Each individual person must choose this life for him or herself and enter into it, but this life cannot be lived in isolation from others who are living this life with God. God meant that they should need each other and Him in the fostering of this life. There are different components of this life that are necessary to its success.

The first is that I be the center of this life, for I am the way. One enters this life through me, and this life is deepened through me. The way brings you and each person who is "in it" to the Father. All this is through and with God, through His power and through my presence. Just as you are asked to walk with me in these words, so too is the whole church asked to walk with me. The "living stones" that make it up come from living daily with me and being led by me. In all this, the love of the Father is made known and is experienced repeatedly within the community. When the whole nation is in communion with God, the fullness of the kingdom of God on earth will be experienced in joy, love, and justice.

But this life is built one person at a time, one community at a time, one nation at a time. This building process requires people who will enter this life with me, and it requires people who know what this life is about and can proclaim its message to all. And in the midst of this is human weakness, error, inconsistency, ignorance, complacency, and laziness. If you could see the difficulties that humans suffer in living this life and passing it on, you would understand what power is at work in preserving and expanding the church. Nonetheless, it is the same life that has been offered from Pentecost on, and this life is constantly being discovered and renewed. The church has learned the depth of this life through the centuries. You are part of this global enterprise of eternal life. You are part of its transmission to others because you have entered into life with me.

Do not think you have to know everything about eternal life or that you have to become a master in describing it to others. Share what you experience of God and how you have come to understand the Father and me through your daily life with me. Share with others how being in this life has given you a grasp of spiritual reality and what it is that God seeks for everyone. Don't think you have to become a professional religious educator to do this work of building the kingdom of God. It is the witness of your life with me and the fruit of this life that is the key.

This is how the kingdom is spread, how the church is built, and how the communion of saints grows. See this communion as comprised of all the living and dead who are in communion with God and one another, and know they work together toward the spread of God's kingdom on earth. Know the joy of being a child of God, His beloved, and know that all are the object of God's love. Invite all, as you are able, to know this life for themselves.

Of course, this work needs structure. Human beings need structure to accomplish their goals. God needs a structure through which His goals are accomplished as well. He needs people who can teach, who can lead, who can proclaim the Word with clarity, who can minister to the people of God, who can be the backbone of the living church. God needs order in the church.[111] God is a God of order and propriety. Heaven is not founded on chaos. Eternal life is comprehensible, and what is needed to enter into it and to flourish in it is known. This is passed on now from generation to generation throughout the world because it is comprehensible and made known.

---

111   1 Corinthians 14:40. "Let everything be done with propriety and in order."

The church needs its leaders and teachers but it cannot remain a church only of those who lead and teach. It needs those who are in the world to be in the world for Christ, to be in the world as children of God who know what this life means and are living it. The witness of the lived life is the potent means by which others come to desire this life with God, come to know that it exists and see potential for themselves in those who are faithful to the love of God.

To see what this means in specific terms, terms that are specific to you and your daily life, let us look at your life and those with whom you live your daily life. This is your part of the kingdom. This is where God has planted you, the garden in which you are to be a visible flower for all to see. What others see *in* you and *of* you is what will draw others to God or deflect others from God.

When you live your life daily with me, this is the basis of the real impact you will have on the others around you. But know that the seed that is in you will have different receptions. Some seed will fall on the edge of the path and be trampled on. Some will fall on rock and will wither away. Some will fall among thorns and be choked. But some will fall on rich soil and grow and produce its crop a hundredfold.[112]

Don't be influenced by the seed that falls anywhere other than fertile soil, but know that there is fertile soil onto which your seed is falling. Do not be concerned about the time it may take for the seed to bear its fruit. This is God's business, and it is He who brings the seed to fruition. This is His work. When you live your life daily with me, I am producing the fruit in your own soul that will bear its fruit in other souls. This is the work of God. Be joyful that you have a part in it. I am the vine; you are

112   Luke 8:5–8

the branches. Whoever remains in me and with me in Him bears fruit in plenty, for you can do nothing when you are cut off from me. Anyone who does not remain in me will wither.[113] And when this happens, the fruit of God cannot be brought into being. God has chosen to act through people in bringing about His kingdom.

When a seed falls into unfertile soil, it doesn't necessarily mean that all is lost. In each person there is a need for God. God Himself has implanted that seed in each soul. Many times this need for God is replaced by other things and becomes so hidden in the person that it seems unreachable. And yet there are events or words that do move a person to realize that there is something so much more valuable in life than what is being lived, and this provides the opportunity for a seed to bear fruit in the soul of the person. The combination of the previous seed and the current seed provide a kind of awakening for the person, and many will act on this opportunity when it arises. You'll never know when this process will happen, but when it happens to somebody who knows you, you will be the model that shows him or her that a connection with God is possible. Sometimes the seed will be planted through you. Sometimes you will be the one the newly awakened one will come to.

People often ask why the kingdom of God is so difficult to bring about. It's because God is seeking what is real, not something that can be acted out or feigned. It is real life with Him that bears real fruit for Him, and this is difficult for human beings. Today, it is particularly difficult because there is so much opposition to religious life in this world. This has occurred in part because so much evil

---

113   John 15:5–6

has been done in the name of religion. There has been so much hypocrisy exposed in those who were presumed to be religious. And then there are the difficulties faced by each person, difficulties that tempt each to give up the effort to be in communion with God. These difficulties can include tragedy, loss of work or home, breakdown of relationship, or the heartbreak of a rebellious child.

All these can cause people to be exhausted and lose their perspective. But this is not the time to give up on God but to come closer to Him, for He is the help in all these situations that arise in life. Come to me, all you who labor and are overburdened, and I will give you rest. Shoulder my yoke and learn from me, for I am gentle and humble in heart, and you will find rest for your souls! Yes, my yoke is easy, and my burden light.[114] And this is when you will find what a help I am and what a loving Father your God is. It is through these difficult times in particular that you will find that your God walks with you, guides you, and sees you through. In these times, your faith is strengthened.

But hear what I said, "My yoke is easy, and my burden light." Think of what my burden was, both when I was preaching the kingdom and had no place to rest my head[115] and when I suffered what God had willed for me. And yet I say that my yoke was easy and my burden light. With God, when it comes to following His will, there is no burden that can overcome you, no event that can destroy you. For everything that God leads you to, He provides the means to triumph in the task and the spiritual strength to see it through to the end. This is His way, and it is the way of His love that becomes revealed to you through what He has

---

114   Matthew 11:28–30
115   Matthew 8:20. "Foxes have holes and the birds of the air have nests, but the Son of Man has nowhere to lay his head."

called you to live. Trust in Him, and trust in me. Indeed, all this builds the "muscle" of your faith, because you come to know that God is with you every moment and that God is leading and sustaining you.

Even so, this is what I am calling you to, for the Lord of heaven and earth is your God and He is the one who seeks to build His kingdom through you. The greatest decision for you to make is actually the first decision you have to make, and that is to give your life to me, to give your life over to God so that His will and love may be fully realized in you. This is the decision I am asking you to make. The rest will take care of itself, for from the moment you place your life in my hands, I begin to work out God's will for you.

Know that He will love you and that you will know His love all the days of your life. Know that you are His and that His grace will be with you and flow through you to others all the days of your life. Know that others will come to know God as you do because of your daily life with me and with the Father through the Holy Spirit. There is no greater calling in life than what you are being called to now. You are being called to the real life with God, a life for which there is no substitute and no equal. You will come to live your life in total trust of God, in total communion with Him, and you will know His heart and His mind.

And you will have friends to share this life with. This will be one of your greatest treasures—to know others who love God and who know His love for them. This will be a surprising source of strength and assurance. But even more than this, as a result of sharing of your life with God, you will see that God is actively building His kingdom through His people. Seek out this communion with others and come to know the love of God through friends who love Him.

One last thing about the mission of the church and your mission: Although I say the laborers are few,[116] I mean this in relationship with the total need. But in the church, there are many faithful servants who have entered this life with God totally. They have entered into holiness, and it is through them primarily that the Lord builds His kingdom, for it is holiness of life that bears the fruit God intends. You will come to know many of these faithful souls who toil for God in His vineyard. And you will be one of them.

But there is another part that you will know along the way. In the parable of the talents, the man who received five talents promptly went and traded with them and made five more. When the master heard this, he told the servant, "Well done, good and faithful servant! You have shown you can be faithful in small things, I will trust you with greater; come and join in your master's happiness."[117] This is how it is with God. He will develop you as His disciple. He will show you how to be a disciple who can be trusted with the things of the kingdom, and He will call you to do greater things for Him. As I said at the last supper: "I tell you most solemnly whoever believes in me will perform the same works as I do myself, he will perform even greater works, because I am going to the Father."[118]

Join now in your master's happiness. This is the joy you will know. You will know the joy in your Father's heart. This is a joy the world cannot give. It is a joy that marks the very life with God that is part of eternal life. Know His love. Know His will. Know His joy. And know the peace I give to you, which no man can take away. This is the life God gives those who are His in mind, heart, and spirit.

---

116   Luke 10:2
117   Matthew 25:21
118   John 14:12

This is your great calling. Enter into this life with me each day, and all these things I have said will come to pass in your own life, in your own flesh and blood.

Chapter 10

～

THE END

The end I speak of now is twofold: the end of time for the world and the end of time for you and each of your loved ones. Let me first review some of the things I have said about the end of time. It is that time when I shall return to bring my own home with me and to separate my flock from those I don't know. This is a hard reality that people find difficult to accept—that God would actually leave some who have rejected Him in their lifetime out of His heavenly kingdom for all time. Let me state again what the spiritual reality is: There are those who will come into heaven and those who will not. Those who will not come into heaven will not cease to be but will exist forever outside the presence of God. The knowledge of this reality will be theirs, and the result will be "weeping and gnashing of teeth," for there can be no greater joy than that known to those who are with God, a foretaste of which is available in this life, and no greater pain than that known to those separated eternally from God.

Those who fear being left out are right to so fear; their fear is rational. Even though I want you to choose God because of His love and desire for you, there are many who have approached God out of fear of being left out of heaven. And they, too, knew the mercy and love of God. Listen to the account of the rich man and Lazarus and take it to heart as the depiction of the reality of the spiritual afterlife.

"There was a rich man who used to dress in purple and fine linen and feast magnificently every day. And at his gate there lay a poor man called Lazarus, covered with sores, who longed to fill himself with the scraps that fell from the rich man's table. Dogs even came and licked his sores. Now the poor man died and was carried away to the bosom of Abraham. The rich man also died and was buried.

"In his torment in Hades he looked up and saw Abraham a long way off with Lazarus in his bosom. So he cried out, 'Father Abraham, pity me and send Lazarus to dip the tip of his finger in water and cool my tongue, for I am in agony in these flames.' 'My son,' Abraham replied, 'remember that during your life good things came your way, just as bad things came the way of Lazarus. Now he is being comforted here while you are in agony. But that is not all: between us and you a great gulf has been fixed, to stop anyone, if he wanted to, crossing from our side to yours, and to stop any crossing from your side to ours.'

"The rich man replied, 'Father, I beg you then to send Lazarus to my father's house, since I have five brothers, to give them warning so that they do not come to this place of torment too.' 'They have Moses and the prophets,' said Abraham, 'let them listen to them.' 'Ah no, father Abraham,' said the rich man, 'but if someone comes to them from the dead, they will repent.' Then Abraham said to him, 'If they will not listen to Moses or the prophets, they will not be convinced even if someone should rise from the dead.'"[119]

And again, I told of how I would come and separate the goats from the sheep. "When the Son of Man comes in glory, escorted by all the angels, then he will separate men from one another as the shepherd separates sheep from goats. He will place the sheep on his right and the goats on his left. Then the King will say to those on his right hand, 'Come, you whom my Father has blessed, take for your heritage the kingdom prepared for you since the foundation of the world. For I was hungry and you gave me food; naked and you clothed me, sick and you visited me, in prison and you came to see me. Next he will say to those on his left hand, 'Go away from me, with your curse upon you, to the eternal fire prepared for the devil and his angels.' And they will go away to eternal punishment, and the virtuous to eternal life."[120]

Compare these depictions to this image of heaven. All those in heaven will be in full view of God their Father. All will be filled with unending joy in His presence. Love will abound, and the gifts of love will be given. Know that what I said is the truth —all who separate themselves from

---

119   Luke 16:19–31
120   Matthew 25:31–46

God will be separated eternally from Him. This follows as night follows the day. But to the faithful will be said these words: "Come, you whom my Father has blessed, take for your heritage the kingdom prepared for you since the foundation of the world."

But this is an image of the time when I will come again at the end of time. There is also that end of time for each person. At that time, I will meet each person, and those who will join me in heaven will do so on that same day just as the good thief did. Others will enter a period of purification before they join me. And others will be refused entry based on their lives and separation from God. I want to speak now of that time when we will meet face-to-face.

This invitation to walk with me daily has everything to do with the end. The people who have walked faithfully with me each day will know what it is to be welcomed by the heavenly hosts in the heavenly kingdom. They will know the immediate joy of seeing God face-to-face. Their Father will welcome them, as will all those whom they have known and helped who have gone before. They won't even know many of these people, but each will come to rejoice in their lives because of what these people did for them. Those in heaven will have their chance to give thanks.

There will be family members who have gone on before, generations of family members who had some part to play in the faith of the loved one now entering heaven. There will be the angels who have looked after them over the course of their lives. There will be all the persons who had a role in the faith development of the person. And then will come the saints who formed the faith of the church over the centuries and the martyrs who gave their lives for me. Joy will be what marks each encounter. All will rejoice at how God has worked in each life, and all will worship the Father for His love.

When you come to that last part of your life, ask me to grant you a peaceful death surrounded by your loved ones. This is a time of great grace for all who know and love you and a time of great grace for you as well. It is a time when you can begin to let go of all your earthly concerns and get all these matters in order so that you can separate yourself from them and leave them to others. This is a time for you to come close to me, and it is a time when I will especially be with you, preparing you for the end and your meeting with me. I will let you know what is awaiting you so that you can be filled with joy at that prospect. This is a joy you won't really be able to share fully with everyone, but you will be able to share enough so that they will know that you have died in grace. And in the end, this will be the great comfort to each of them, especially those who are close to me.

You will have the consolation of knowing that you and I are close and that love cannot have a greater bond in this life than what we now share. This spirit will permeate you, and you will have peace. This truly is the peace no one can take from you. And when the end finally comes and you have entered your eternal rest, you like all the saints will also have the knowledge needed to pray for those you love.

In addition, you will be given special people to pray for. For example, if you have a special love for music, you may be given certain musicians to pray for, or if you are a nurse, you may be given people with certain illnesses to pray for. In each case, you will be praying for specific souls. For most, family members will be the special focus of prayer. The state of the kingdom on earth will continue to be a concern to you. But now you will be able to pray in the full knowledge of what God is asking of you, and it will be your joy to do so.

Think of those you have known who have died in grace. Think of what it meant to you that they did so. Think of the peace it gave you to know they died knowing God. But that wasn't the end of the story. They have continued to pray for you and others since they died. You may be able to think of things that have happened in your life or in the lives of others that you feel certain they must have influenced with their prayers. You would be right in thinking so. This is exactly the nature of the heavenly host. They are active in their intercession for those on earth, just as you intercede with prayers for those you love. You do well to ask the saints to pray for you and for others, for they will do so. The litany of the saints is a wonderful image of this kind of prayer.

Know, too, that I am with them as I am with you. There is no separation in time between when I am with you and when I am with them. I am always with them in their full view. I am always intimately in touch with each of them as I am with you and countless others on earth simultaneously. Do you see the power in this presence with all those who are in communion with me? I am the Lord of the universe, and you have instant and full access to me at a glance. I walk day-by-day with each of my followers. Keep this wonderful image of the fullness of the kingdom of God.

To be a channel of grace now is a foretaste of being a channel of grace in heaven. In the here and now, you are limited in your understanding and in your ability to fully give to others. You are limited in the depth of your knowledge and love of the Father, and you are limited in being a pure vessel for the work of the Holy Spirit. In spite of all this, holiness is within your grasp when you walk daily with me, and you are a channel of grace to others. This means that my life in you is shared in some way with others; others are the beneficiaries of your life with me and of your union with God.

This is an image of what life is like in heaven. Just as the Eucharistic banquet is an image of the heavenly banquet, your life of grace is an image of how grace operates in heaven. But there are significant differences. On earth, you love your Father whom you can't see, but in heaven, there is no such limitation. You will be in full view of your Father and of me. To see God is to be transformed fully into a vessel of love. In heaven you are fully His child in divinity. You are a "divinized human" who retains your identity and your personal character. But now you are a pure, transparent vessel of grace, which means you can give your gifts, now perfected in heaven, to others in heaven as part of the heavenly banquet. And you intercede for others on earth; however, this time, you will know what to ask for, and your prayers will be answered.[121] At the end of time, all in heaven will have their risen, imperishable bodies just as I have mine. In this body, you will move and act and have your being. As Paul said, "The first man, being from the earth, is earthly by nature; the second man is from heaven. As this earthly man was, so are we on earth; and as the heavenly man is, so are we in heaven. And we, who have been modeled on the earthly man, will be modeled on the heavenly man. Or, put it this way: flesh and blood cannot inherit

---

121   John 15:16. I commissioned you to go out and bear fruit, fruit that will last; and then the Father will give you anything you ask him in my name.

the kingdom of God: and the perishable cannot inherit what lasts for ever. I will tell you something that has been a secret: that we are not going to die, we shall all be changed."[122]

In heaven, you will realize far more than you are capable of realizing now—what a wonder the human being is and what it means that man was made in the image of God. God created man in the image of Himself. In the image of God, He created him. Male and female, He created them.[123] Here are images of God to help you see what I am saying here. God is compassionate. Humans can be compassionate, and in heaven, they will fully become the image of God. God is love. Humans can love, and in heaven, they will fully become the image of God. God is merciful. Humans can be merciful, and in heaven, they will fully become the image of God. It is in this mercy that they will pray for those given to them to love from heaven. God thinks rightly. Humans can think rightly, but in heaven, they will fully become God's image. This is the image that man was created in, and through his separation from God, his image of God became disfigured by hatred and jealousy and the like. In heaven, his image of God will be fully restored, and at that time, the joy of seeing man fully alive will be a great source of joy and sharing in heaven.

Think of how the human soul enjoys and appreciates beauty. In heaven, beauty abounds, and the heavenly soul rejoices fully in it. They shall see the beauty of God, a beauty that cannot be described on earth. The goodness of God will be seen in all its glory, and the divinized soul will be able to "take it in."

---

122   1 Corinthians 15:47–51
123   Genesis 1:27

When you are with me each day, keep this larger view of heaven and earth with you so that we can talk of things that fall within this understanding. When you pray for people, those who have gone before and who need your prayers during that time of purification as well as those on earth who need your prayers, call on the heavenly host to assist you in your prayer just as you would ask a friend to pray for someone. Every now and then, ask me to allow you to rest in my heart in such a way that you may take in the spirit of that heavenly kingdom. In other words, don't just rest with me in the here and now but rest with me in eternal life. You can do this because I am with you and because I am totally in eternal life, and you also can be where I am if I permit this presence as I have done with Paul and others.[124] Sometimes I will lead you into my secret place, where I will build you up in ways that no words or other actions can do. Do not exclude these encounters with me from your understanding of life with me.

In these moments of great grace when I am so intimately present with you, know what a great gift I have given you in the Eucharist. There am I, invisible except for the appearance of bread and wine, fully present to you in flesh and blood, body, soul, and divinity. There, too, I do my invisible work in the soul. Love me in that form, and offer me the gift of thanksgiving for my coming into you in that form. There is no greater physical form in which I am present to man. Love me there as I love you.

---

124   2 Corinthians 12:2–5. "I will move on to the visions and revelations I have had from the Lord. I know a man in Christ who, fourteen years ago, was caught up—whether still in the body or out of the body, I do not know; God knows—right into the third heaven. I do know, however, that this same person was caught up into paradise and heard things which must not and cannot be put into human language."

And now, as we bring this part of our walk to a conclusion, know that I am with you until the end of time, your time on earth. I will walk with you each day. Set time aside to be with me. Discover how to be with me profitably. The church knows how you can do this. Never become discouraged in being with me. Know deep within yourself that I am with you every moment. Develop the habit of turning to me often during the day and bringing me into all your situations each day. Develop these habits until they become second nature to you. Let what is in this little walk be a "backbone" of your understanding of me, and grow from here through being with me, hearing what I say, studying what I did, relating to my actions in your life, and living this life daily.

Pray to your Father as I have taught you and will teach you. When you think of me, think of Him as one with me. Increasingly know His love for you and all those who are in me, and all those who could be. Hold those I give you in prayer and love. Love the church that continues my work throughout the earth and pray for its leaders and teachers so that they may be faithful to me. Pray for more laborers in the vineyard of the Lord,[125] and pray for your whole family so that all may know God. Unite with me in spirit and truth and live the abundant life of grace I give you.

Bow your head now and receive my blessing.

---

125   Luke 10:2

CPSIA information can be obtained at www.ICGtesting.com
Printed in the USA
LVOW050727270213

321809LV00001B/10/P